CROSS ROADS
REFLECTIONS

Reflections
for Every Day
of the Year

"Life is bigger than death!"

CROSS ROADS REFLECTIONS

Reflections for
Every Day of the Year

WM. PAUL YOUNG

FaithWords
New York • Boston • Nashville

Cover and interior design by Koechel Peterson and Associates, Inc., Minneapolis, Minnesota

FaithWords
Hachette Book Group USA
237 Park Avenue
New York, NY 10017

Visit our website at www.faithwords.com.

Printed in the United States of America

First Edition: September 2013

10 9 8 7 6 5 4 3 2 1

Library of Congress Control Number: 2013938451

To our "Clans"
Warren, Young
Boyle, Bruneski, Johnson, Landis,
Racanelli, Sparrow, Steele

So thankful for you all,
and all you have been to us!
Our roots are deep and strong,
Down into the River of Life,
The Tree now bearing fruit for healing!

A NOTE TO THE READER

Thank you for picking up this book of Reflections, a journey of encountering various Cross Roads and responding, or not, to their implicit invitation to stop, listen, and take the risks involved in transformational change. This is not intended to be a "daily devotional" in the traditional sense. I love such books—Oswald Chambers' *My Utmost for His Highest*, being one of my favorites, or the writings of F. W. Boreham.

This book of Reflections is a different sort of journey. Each month has an overarching theme and raises questions and conversations within that theme. It follows the arc of the story line in Anthony Spencer's life, the main character in the novel *Cross Roads*, and therefore you will recognize a movement over the course of the year. Sometimes the connections will be quite subtle, such as a word that can also be defined as "vague," but it is not my job nor within the scope of my abilities to make the connections from words and questions to your heart and soul and mind. That I respectfully and gratefully leave to the Holy Spirit, who is a redeeming genius.

We are all living in the same world of wonder and wounded, but often it seems as though we each inhabit a different universe, parallel and intersecting and yet wholly and holy our own. We are designed by and for community and yet also intended to be alone and distinct. Both are celebrated, and both are important and good, part of the great dance into which we have been created and included. Perhaps we ought not to be surprised that this rhythm and movement creates such beauty and such tension, but we often are exactly that—amazed, dismayed, joyful, torn, and we vacillate between light and dark. This book is an attempt to celebrate all of that, especially the penetration into the "ordinary" of everything that is extra-ordinary until you cannot distinguish the one from the other.

Sometimes the reflection is for you to see yourself and ask the questions that might arouse some deeper self-awareness. At other times, it may be for another—someone you love or someone you are trying to forgive or even someone you hardly know. Both are calls to prayer, a slowly emerging prayer over the course of the year, a conversation inside a relationship that involves speaking and listening. It will always include "an other," visible or invisible, an expression of Aloneness and Community. In these words, I trust that you will know that should I see you along life's journey, *my desire is to be with you, to not cross the road and pass you by. You matter—to me, to the cosmos, to God.*

WM. PAUL YOUNG, Author of *Cross Roads*

1 JANUARY

The Month of Dismay

The idea of actual change was daunting. The more entrenched in his habits and securities, the less inclined he was to believe that anything else was worth the effort if even possible. Known routines, even though painful at times, at least had their own predictability.

I do like the "idea" of change; it has a romantic air of challenge and wonder. My experience of actual change has often been painful and messy. I suppose it is easier to stay inside my lonely house and dream about change. Can I tell you that I really don't like loneliness, but in time the oldest shirts become the most comfortable?

2

All was quiet as if the world was holding her breath. There are many ways to be alone.

Please teach me the difference between lonely and alone, how to move away from the isolation of lonely but into the embrace of the alone. Wait, on second thought, I think I will stay with lonely for a while longer. While it might not be a good friend, it's at least someone I know.

3 JANUARY

He was determined and ever in search of the next advantage. That often required an outgoing and gregarious presence, broad smiles, eye contact, and firm handshakes, not because of any true consideration, but because everyone potentially held information that would be valuable in positioning for success. His many questions created the aura of genuine interest, leaving others with both a sense of significance but also a lingering emptiness.

I am such a Jacob at times—
manipulator, usurper, scrambler. . . .
I want to become authentic. . . . I just
don't know how to get there. Please?

4

Known for gestures of philanthropy, he understood the value of compassion as a means to more important objectives. Caring made people that much easier to manipulate.

The means justify the ends, the means justify the ends, the means . . . What a diabolical lie, especially when the ends are all wrong to begin with. I confess that I don't even know how to do the right thing with the right motives. I need you to change my heart!

5 JANUARY

After a few halting attempts he has concluded that friends of any depth were a bad investment. So little return. Actual caring was inconvenient and a luxury for which he had no time or energy.

I did try the friend thing . . . you remember. Didn't work out so well. If I recall, I wanted them to be "perfect" friends, everything I needed them to be for me, not real people. I keep getting invited into relationships and I keep resisting, staying safe, and staying lonely. What are you trying to say to me?

6

For Tony, happiness was a silly and transient sentiment, a vapor compared to the smell of a potential deal and the addicting aftertaste of the win. Like Scrooge of old, he took delight in wresting the last vestiges of dignity from those around him, especially employees who toiled from fear if not respect.

It's only a game, right? Life is a reality video game where you have to compete to get to the next level. People are obstacles and impediments. I need to know that there are more levels or maybe a better reason to keep playing. Thoughts?

7

That marriage had ended in divorce for irreconcilable differences, a poster story of calculated disaffection and a callous lack of consideration. In only a few short years Tony had battered Loree's sense of worth and value into barely recognizable bits and pieces.

I am so skilled at self-justification, which I suppose is the way I understand my salvation. I can create language that makes the evil I perpetrate into something noble, or at least . . . justifiable. In moments of honesty, it makes me sick.

JANUARY 8

The price he paid was losing his daughter in the process, something that rose like a specter in the shadows of a little too much Scotch, a little haunting that could soon be buried in the busyness of work and winning.

Is there anything sadder than
the loss of your daughter's smile?
I need to get back to work . . .

9 JANUARY

If freedom is an incremental process, so, too, is the encroachment of evil. Small adjustments to truth and minor justifications over time build an edifice that would never have been predicted.

In our isolation, it is easier to see
in the mirror an angel of light.

10

The inside house of the soul is magnificent but fragile; any betrayals and lies embedded in its walls and foundation shift its construction in directions unimagined.

How did I get here . . . from there? I would have said it was impossible, but here I am, successful in ways that don't even matter. I am so good at lying to myself that I don't know what is actually true. Do you think I might need people in my life who will tell me the truth? . . . No! . . . Wait . . .

11 JANUARY

The mystery of every human soul,
even Anthony Spencer, is profound.

Please open my eyes to see, especially in the despicable, the damaging, the callous, the uncaring, the hurtful, the unkind . . . this profound mystery, the beauty of the human soul whom you love!

12

He had been birthed in an explosion of life, an inner expanding universe coalescing its own internal solar systems and galaxies with unimagined symmetry and elegance. Here even chaos played her part and order emerged as a by-product. Places of substance entered the dance of competing gravitational forces, each adding their own rotation to the mix, shifting the members of the cosmic waltz and spreading them out in a constant give-and-take of space and time and music.

. . . and here, I believed I was an accident, an inconvenience, a loss. . . . I think I am a believer, after all, in lies.

13 JANUARY

Along this road, pain and loss came crushing, causing this depth to lose its profoundly delicate structure and begin to collapse in on itself. The deterioration rippled on the surface in self-protective fear, selfish ambition, and the hardening of anything tender.

What was I supposed to do? Sure, I made choices that hurt, but so much I never wanted or asked for and was not in my control. Are you surprised by what I have become? Disappointed? What was I supposed to do?

14

What had been a living entity, a heart of flesh, became stone; a small hardened rock lived in the husk, the shell of the body. Once the form was an expression of inward wonder and magnificence. Now it must find its way with no support, a facade in search of a heart, a dying star ravenous in its own emptiness.

I confess to you, I don't know how to turn a heart of stone into a heart of flesh. I'm not sure I want to go through what it takes. Please be my courage. I know I can't do this by myself.

15

Pain, loss, and finally abandonment are each a hard taskmaster, but combined they become a desolation almost unendurable. These had weaponized Tony's existence, equipping him with the ability to hide knives inside words, erect walls protecting the within from any approach, and keeping him locked in an imagination of safety while isolated and solitary.

My whole life has become an exercise in staying "safe." Lonely feels safer than exposed, isolation than relationship . . . and yet . . .

JANUARY 16

Little true music now existed in Tony's life; scraps of creativity barely audible. The soundtrack of his subsistence didn't even qualify as Muzak—unsurprising elevator melodies accompanying his predictable elevator pitches.

I know that my incessant desire for self-protection has reduced my ability to experience life and emotions, and I hardly know what loving might look like. But if you heal my heart, will I have to actually "feel" again? Can I tell you how terrifying that sounds to me?

17 JANUARY

Fawning sycophants awaited his next directive, desperate to win a scrap of approval or perceived affection. In the wake of alleged success, others are carried along by a need to secure their own significance, identity, and agenda. Perception is reality, even if the perception is a lie.

Sometimes people make me sick, the way they use me to try to feel better, to step on me as a way of getting what they think they need, to find some certainty and security. Okay, I just realized that is what I do, too, and I'm a little sick of myself. Help?

18

What began as a hint of a shadow of uneasiness had grown to a conscious voice.

I hardly dare thank you for the unease in my life, the dismay that calls into question the ways I protect myself. I'm afraid you might take my gratitude as a request to make this permanent. I'm hoping you know me better than that and maybe that you care about me . . . even a little.

19 JANUARY

The more he looked, the more he noticed, so the more he looked. He had always been a little paranoid, but it now escalated to constant considerations of conspiracy, and he lived agitated and unnerved.

Why is it that I am so much more disposed to creating and living in an imagination that I am being wronged than in taking the risk to find out that I might be mistaken. I would even sacrifice long-term relationships to this imagination. Do you really love people like me, who are a little crazy?

20

He kept a collection of vinyl records whose scratches were like comforting reminders of times long gone.

Thank you for little bits of my history that occasionally show up; small reminders that there were other times, moments of innocence and wonder and simplicity. These call to me still. Thank you!

21 JANUARY

He frequently reviewed and changed [his official Last Will and Testament], adding or subtracting people as they intersected his life and their actions angered or pleased him. He imagined the impact of a gift or the lack thereof on those who would care about his wealth once he had joined the ranks of the "dearly departed."

I confess I keep such a document in my imagination, and I add or erase people as they please or hurt me. It's rather a sick pleasure, being able to control others without being embarrassed about it, and it's not a way I would want others to think about me.

22

He had burned bridges, most bridges actually, and he supposed that therein he would find the answers. *It has to be about money,* he surmised. Wasn't everything about money?

Money has been my god, something tangible that I could center my life around to give me a sense of certainty, worth, value, significance, and security. Its absence empowers my fears as does its presence, and it always challenges relationships. I need your wisdom.

23

He was currently the office hero, but this did not give him much peace. Any respite would be short-lived, and every success simply raised the bar of performance expectations. It was an exhausting way to live, but he resisted other options as irresponsible and lazy.

When burdens become our friends,
any freedom seems irresponsible.

JANUARY 24

When uncertainty impinges upon routine, one begins to think about one's life as a whole, about who matters and why.

I love uncertainty! I hate uncertainty!
I love that it shakes me loose from the
moorings of control and pushes me deeper.
I hate that it is so . . . uncertain.

25 JANUARY

He was alone, but most of the time preferred it . . . He had reached every objective he had set, at least every realistic goal, and now in his forties he survived with a brooding sense of emptiness and percolating regrets. These he quickly stuffed down inside, into that invisible vault that human beings create to protect themselves from themselves.

In all my stuffing, I have become two people, and I am finding myself increasingly hard to live with. If you care for me, would you please find both of me and put me back together?

26

It was then that the idea occurred to create a list of those he trusted. Not of people he would say he trusted, but those he actually did trust. Those he would tell secrets to, share dreams with, and with whom he would expose his weaknesses.

Learning to trust an "other" is the true journey for every human being, but especially for those betrayed as children. Performance, be it religious or otherwise, is safer and easily justifiable; it makes everything about me.

27 JANUARY

The only people he truly trusted were all dead . . .

Dear God, I need some living people in my life whom I can trust. Please help me find them, or help them find me.

28

He treasured the faded photograph, the last one taken before a teenage partyer lost control and turned glory into rubble. He opened the safe and pulled it out, now protected inside a laminated sheet, but he tried to smooth out its wrinkles anyway, as if caressing it could somehow let them know.

I have people who showed up in
a particular moment of my need.
Some day, would you please let
me tell them, thank them?

29 JANUARY

It was enough,
his father's grin.

*How can something so simple,
so ordinary, have such power?*

30

Why had he written down the names of these people? It had been almost without thought, this final list, perhaps a true reflection of a source very deep and maybe even real, perhaps even a *longing*. He detested that word, but loved it somewhere. It sounded weak on the surface, but it had sure staying power, outlasting most other things that had come and gone in his life.

Something in this longing tells me that there is more to me, to us, than we know, someone larger and more alive, regardless of how I pretend it is not so and try to justify its removal.

31

These three iconic personages represented, along with the last name on the list, something larger than himself, a hint of a song never sung but still calling, the possibility of someone he might have been, an invitation, a belonging, a tender *yearning*.

> *I want to believe that there is a "bigger" that gives meaning to what is and to what I have made, even in my best efforts. I need to know that I matter just as I am, but that I belong to something or someone who cares.*

1 FEBRUARY

The Month of Undoing

The last name was the most difficult and yet the easiest: Jesus. Jesus, Bethlehem's gift to the world, the woodworker who supposedly was God joining our humanity, who might not be dead, according to the religious rumors.

Jesus! In some ways I would prefer that you were a dead hero and great model, whom we could read and talk about in museums. That way I wouldn't have to actually trust you or consider how, if you are God who joined us in our humanity, that changes everything.

2

"I felt joy. I felt like my heart was about to burst out of my chest. Tony, I am so thankful to God for you."

Thank you for joy, even though it is quite an intrusion at times, messing with my sarcasm and pessimism. It shows up unexpected and surprises me. Is it a reminder that you are here?

3 FEBRUARY

"Hold on to Jesus, Anthony. You can never go wrong by holding on to Jesus. And know this," she said as she pulled back and looked up into his eyes. "He will never stop holding on to you."

Jesus, if you are truly holding on to me,
it means that I am, and that I will be,
and that I matter. Please help my unbelief.

4

The necklace still lay in his safe. He had never given it away. Had she known? He had often wondered if this had been a premonition, some warning or gesture by God to give him a remembrance.

I don't pretend that I understand how things are interconnected, or how you work inside the mass of choices we are all making, but I have seen too much to write it off as chance or karma or fate or luck. Please help me become a child again, one who can see.

5 FEBRUARY

Her loss had destroyed his life, sending it careening down a path that had made him who he was, strong, tough, and able to withstand things that others struggled with. But there were moments, fleeting and intangible, when the tender longing would slip in between the rocks of his presentation and sing to him, or begin to sing as he would quickly shut such music away.

Please be stronger and kinder than the systems I have constructed in my heart that keep me lost.

6

Was Jesus still holding him? Tony didn't know, but probably not.

When my "truster" got shattered, I know it extended to everyone, including you, and I can't help but interpret every nuance as evidence that isolation is safer. I am stuck, and I don't know how to move from here. Please help.

7

He felt that Jesus had said good-bye like everyone else.

Somewhere deep inside of me, I am desperate to hope that you, Father, Son, and Holy Spirit, don't do abandonment.

FEBRUARY 8

What wasn't there to like about [Jesus]? A man's man, yet good with children, kind to those unacceptable to religion and culture, a person full of infectious compassion, someone who challenged the status quo and yet loved those he challenged. He was everything that Tony sometimes wished he was, but knew he wasn't.

Jesus, if you are a model for me to strive to be like, you need to look somewhere else. I'm just too broken to compete. I will always be a disappointment. It would be great news if you are more than that.

9 FEBRUARY

Perhaps Jesus was an example of that bigger-than-yourself life, but it was too late to change. The older he got, the thought of transformation seemed increasingly remote.

I suppose that is the trap; the more time I have to pile up the damages I have caused, the harder it is to face it. Shame means I only have the ability to look at the ground, and I don't even know where I am going. Please tell me it is possible to change.

10

Tony had long decided that if there was a God, he or she or it was something or someone terrible and malevolent, capricious and untrustworthy, at best some form of cold dark matter, impersonal and uncaring, and at worst a monster taking pleasure in devastating the hearts of children.

"Good souls many will one day be horrified at the things they now believe of God."
—George MacDonald

11 FEBRUARY

Living people couldn't be trusted. Reaching for a fresh bottle of Balvenie Portwood, he poured himself a triple . . .

Hah! A triple! That is where I go for comfort rather than trust a trinity of Relentless Affection. Cheers? Not likely, but my addictions at least take the edge off the pain, even if only for a moment.

12

As he sat in the darkness thinking about his existence . . .

I am praying that this darkness, the
primal womb, the abyss of nonbeing,
is a greater lie than my existence.
Is there light where there is no darkness?
Please remember that I am blind.

13 FEBRUARY

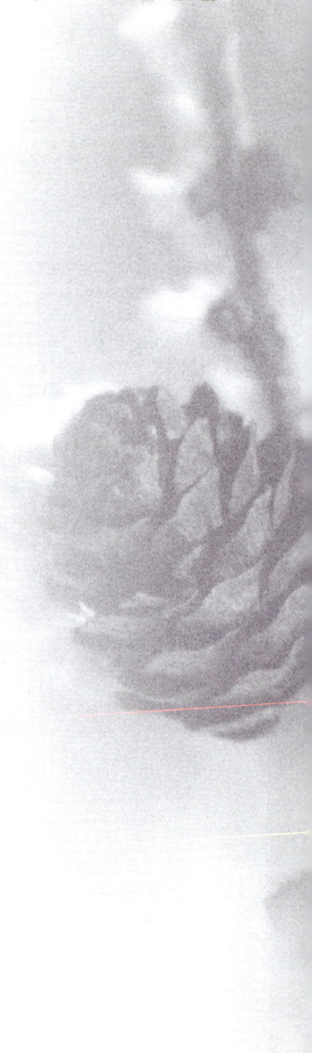

Tony felt raw fear, long imprisoned by sheer willful determination, now bursting its bonds like a beast, feeding off expanding uncertainty.

I might not know love, but I know fear. It is my abusive lover who defines everything for me, who shames me for my lack of control and perfection and respects me not one bit. Are you a love that would cast it out?

14

As he rose, an inner suggestion emerged that he was dying, and the thought easily anchored itself. Internally, he braced as if he might have the power to resist being absorbed into . . . what? Nothingness? Was he merging with the impersonal all-spirit?

No. He had long decided that death was the simple end, the cessation of all conscious awareness, dust relentlessly returning to dust.

If death is not the final answer,
then life itself must be the
question. I am asking . . .

15

When all was said and done, wasn't he justified in looking out for himself, controlling not only his life but also others' lives for his benefit and advantage? There was no single right thing, no absolute truth, just legislated social mores and guilt-based conformity.

If there is no true Truth, then nothing matters, and I am completely undone! I have known no greater despair than when hope itself was not a possibility.

FEBRUARY 16

Death as he viewed it meant that nothing truly mattered. Life was a violent evolutionary gasp of meaninglessness, the temporary survival of the smartest or most cunning. A thousand years from now, providing the human race survived, no one would know he had even existed or care how he lived his life.

And yet, I live as if something or someone matters. I find this conflicting desire to move toward authenticity, to accept the invitation of relationship, as if they matter. Please tell me, does anything matter?

17 FEBRUARY

On one specific day, hope for anything more had died. That stormy November morning, for almost a minute, he held the first shovelful of dirt. Standing in wind-driven rain, he stared down at the small ornate box that held his Gabriel. Barely five years old and hardly a breath, his little boy had fought courageously to hold on to everything beautiful and good, only to be torn from the tenderness of the ones who loved him most.

Why is it that children naturally bend toward light and love, toward wonder and goodness, toward creativity and kindness? Is it wrong to want to be such a child again, one day?

18

Tony finally let the soil fall into that abyss. Shattered bits of his broken heart tumbled in also, along with any remaining scraps of hope. But no tears. Rage against God, against the machine, against even the decay in his own soul, had not saved or kept his son. Begging, promises, prayers, all bounced off the sky and returned empty, mocking his impotence. Nothing . . . nothing had made any difference as Gabriel's voice went silent.

Is there anything worse than losing a child?

19 FEBRUARY

But what did any of it matter anyway? Wishful thinking, that was the real foe. The what-if, or what could have been or should have been or might have been, was all a sucking waste of energy and an impediment to success and in-the-moment self-gratification.

When I encounter those wounds too deep to bleed and the raw fury of my impotence, I just want to bury it somehow, to feel nothing, to comfort myself with whatever is at hand. I don't know what I'm doing, and I pray you understand.

20

The very idea that anything mattered was a lie, a delusion, a false comfort as one drifted toward the ax. Once annihilated, what remained of him would be the illusions of those still living, retaining temporary but fleeting recollections, bad or good, all momentary bits of a mirage that his life had significance.

I suppose my confession is that if I believe one thing matters, then everything matters. . . . Does that make me a believer? Just asking . . .

21 FEBRUARY

Since hope was a myth,
it could not be an enemy.

No, death was death and
that was the final word.

I pray that there is a word,
a final word that is not ours,
but yours!

22

It was an invitation to take a deep breath, and when he did he could almost taste the scents, strong and savory with barely a touch of salt in the wind as if an ocean lay just beyond the range of sight.

Just when I think I have everything nailed down, some hint of life shows up from somewhere and ruins everything. Thank you?

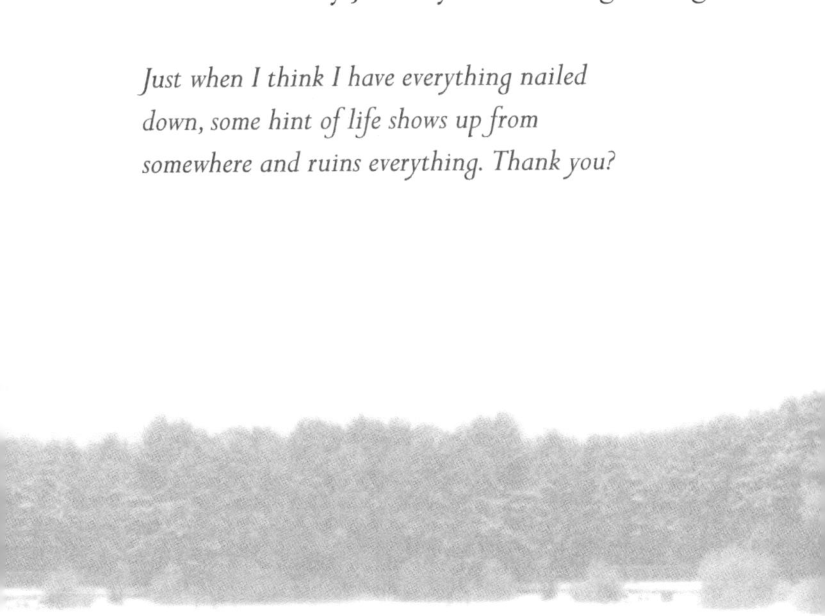

23

Tony stood absolutely still, as if that would help quiet the storm inside his head. His thoughts were a cascade of confusion. Was he dreaming or insane? Was he dead? Obviously not, unless . . . unless he was completely wrong about death, a thought too disconcerting to take seriously.

I have been such a stickler for being right about everything that I haven't considered how being wrong about something could open up a world of possibilities. Then again . . . I could be wrong about that . . . wait . . .

FEBRUARY 24

He turned back to the cave, startled to see that it had vanished, absorbed back into the wall of granite without a trace. That option removed, he was down to only one obvious choice, the path.

When all escape routes are closed,
we get to be fully present.

25 FEBRUARY

He could smell this world, a mixture of life and decay, the piney dampness of old growth, moldy and yet sweet. Tony took another deep breath, trying to hold the scent. It was almost an intoxication, a remembrance of Scotch, similar to his beloved Balvenie Portwood, but richer, purer, and with a stronger aftertaste.

I catch glimpses or catch a scent . . .
of something just beyond sensing, but
real and having more substance than
my imagination. Could that be you?

26

It is an odd feeling, trying to make a decision about matters where not only the outcomes are unforeseeable, but the present situation is unknown. He didn't know where he had come from, didn't know where he was going, and was now faced with choices with no knowledge of what each might mean or cost.

In those moments when everything is unknown, what emerge are the questions about what I really want. Terrifying? Yes! Good? Yes!

27 FEBRUARY

Life had been a long series of encountered choices, intersections, and he had bluffed his way to decisions, convincing himself and others that he completely understood where each would take them, that each was a simple extension of his own correct evaluations and brilliant judgments.

I wonder, in my house of cards,
how much of my life has been a bluff?

28

Tony had labored diligently to extract certainty out of option, to somehow control the future and its outcomes by exuding an aura of intelligent prophetic prescience. The truth, he now understood, was that eventualities and consequences were never inevitable, and marketing and image-making were the tools of choice to cover the disparity.

I am so tired of the fantasy, all the smoke and mirrors, and all the energy it takes to keep it believable. It wears me out and feeds off of the real life. I am tired!

29 FEBRUARY

for such years as celebrate this da

There were always interfering variables outside the range of probability that muddied the waters of control.

You are the Grand Interferer, the voice from "outside" that reorients everything. If you are truly there in Person, then what I think of as control is at best a myth and at worst, unbelief. But you would know that and take that into consideration, right?

1 MARCH

The Month of Transition

Creating the illusion that he knew and then bluffing became his method of operation. It was a grueling challenge to remain a prophet when things were so unpredictable.

My confession: I want certainty without relationship; I want magic without consequence, and I want formula and expectation without grace and kindness. I'm sick! Is this a surprise to you?

2

He stood facing three choices with not one clue as to where each would lead. Surprisingly, there was an unexpected freedom in not knowing, the absence of any expectation that would eventually find him guilty of a wrong decision. He was free in this moment to pick any direction, and that autonomy was both exhilarating and frightening, a tightrope walk potentially between fire and ice.

Somewhere in the deep places of my soul,
I know that it is the ability to choose that
makes me incomprehensively magnificent and
uniquely dangerous. I cannot do this by myself.

3 MARCH

He felt hopelessly lost, not that he had been found to begin with or had any sense of a destination, which only added to his feeling of bewilderment.

When I am most honest, I would admit that that is what I feel deepest . . . lost. And I don't even know where I am or am going and don't know how to get found. Please come find me!

4

What if it's not about getting anywhere? he wondered. What if there was no goal or objective here? As the pressure to "arrive" eased, Tony unintentionally slowed down and began paying attention to the world around him.

What have I been so busy at, really? I want there to be more times when I willingly give my attention to that which is right in front of me.

5 MARCH

Not having an objective had inherent gifts—no timetable demands and no agendas—and Tony hesitantly allowed the surroundings to begin assuaging the nagging frustration of being so utterly disoriented.

I only know a world of agendas and timetables. Please teach me how to be alive inside of this busy-ness, to be present.

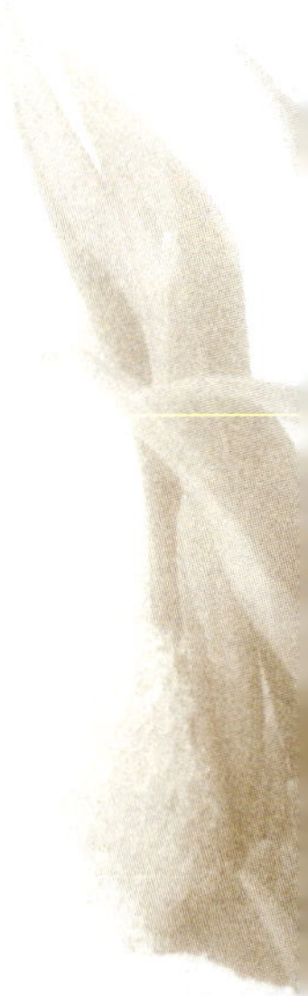

6

One trail took him under a cleft in the rocky face of the mountain, almost but not quite a cave, and he couldn't help but quicken his pace in case this little gap closed and crushed him in a stony grip.

Today is the celebration of Nathan V's healing, when as a seventeen-year-old Down's syndrome young man, he was accidently hit and killed by two cars. If you have read Cross Roads, you know him as Cabby. Sometimes the little gap closes.

7 MARCH

Another choice took him through a scarred area where fire had some time past ripped the heart out of the woods, leaving stubs and relics of the aged along with scatterings of a new generation of tender growth, feeding off the death of the past and emerging to salvage what had been lost, and more.

I don't understand how you are able to take death and grow something living out of it. Help me to be aware of the life rather than so focused on the death.

8

One path merged and followed an ancient and dried sandy riverbed, while another was a barely discernible climb on velvet moss that swallowed his footprints as he passed. But always another crossing, and more alternatives.

Please teach me to be aware of all the intersections and crossings that occur inside each day, the many small choices that ripple through the fabric of my relationships and direction. Thank you for the respect you give us in the choosing.

9

After several hours of hiking, wandering, and wondering, it occurred to Tony that the number of direction decisions was diminishing; options were significantly decreasing. The singular footpath slowly widened into something that could easily be a narrow lane, the trees and brush on either side closing ranks to form an almost impenetrable barrier.

Thank you for those times when options are reduced and the choices narrowed. Please teach me to see that even in those times freedom is undiminished and "being" in the limitations is as wondrous as in the choices.

MARCH 10

He had never been much of a dancer, but here no one could see him, and so there was no chance of embarrassment. If he wanted to dance, he would dance. This was "his" dream, and he possessed the power and authority to do whatsoever he wanted.

There is a child inside that wants to dance, but the adult of culture and heritage and training resists for fear of embarrassment. Free me, please, to be the child!

11 MARCH

While obviously a point of entry, there were no visible means of access, no knob or keyhole, nothing that would allow him admission. It seemed it could be opened only from the inside, which meant that something, or someone, had to be in there to open it.

"Well, this should be interesting," he muttered to himself, and raised his fist to knock. Tony froze! He heard a knock, but it wasn't him; his hand was still raised.

I have so often lived as if existence were inside a closed box. I defined life by the walls, and then I heard a knock . . . from outside . . . and everything changes!

12

He looked back at the door. A clasp had appeared where he hadn't seen one before. How could he have missed it?

I know I live much of my life oblivious to even what is obvious to a child. Please heal my eyes so that I can see. I don't want to keep missing!

13 MARCH

He was already standing inside, looking farther into a sweeping open land, likely more than half a dozen square miles in area. The property was confined inside gigantic stone walls, a boundaried fortress in contrast to the wild and free world outside.

A fortress in the middle of a wild and free creation . . . sounds familiar . . . sounds like me. You know I believe these walls are what saved my life, right?

14

"So"—Tony cleared his throat—"do all those trails end up here?" The question seemed rather shallow, but in the myriad of so many it was the first to surface.

"No," the man answered, his voice strong and resonant. "Quite the opposite, actually. All those paths originate from here. Not often traveled these days."

I know that the damage in my soul has shut me down in terms of authentic relationships, and I'm afraid. You do love people who are afraid, right?

15 MARCH

"Childhood influences have staggering formative consequences, for good and evil, or for life."

I was once a child and roamed these hills
in freedom and abandon, but then an adult
I became and gave up all my wandering. I
now survive within the fortress I so carefully
constructed, with pretty walls and furnishings,
my wonder deconstructed. And if by kindness you
come by, please visit if you're able, for fear has
kept me safe within this cell of chair and table.

16

"Knowing is quite layered. Even our own souls we hardly apprehend until the veils are lifted, until we come out of the hiding and into the place of being known."

Being known . . . that sounds wonderful and scares me to the core. It would mean . . . being known, with all my broken bits and all my layered shame.

17

"Your invitation was many years ago and probably remains at best but a vague feeling or longing for you. If I had thought to bring a book and you could smell its pages, that most assuredly would help, but I didn't."

Thank you for the little things I opened up my heart to as a child. I know that even though I locked most of these away, you didn't lose them.

MARCH 18

"There is indeed a sense that the word *hell* might be an appropriate word for here, but then, so would the word *home*."

Someone has said that a religious person is someone who believes in hell, and a spiritual person is someone who has been there.

19 MARCH

"Tony, what exactly do you think hell is?"

There are questions that you are not supposed to ask, and this is one of those. A better question is "What is the nature of the Person who created hell?". . . and now you are sending me to the principal's office?

20

The question of hell had always been an assumption. As a result, Tony's response came out more a question than a statement. "A place of eternal torment with fire and gnashing of teeth and stuff? . . . Uh, a place where God punishes people he is angry with because they are sinners, . . . where bad people are separated from God and good people go to heaven?"

I confess, I have been wrong about a lot of things, and I am willing to be wrong about this one, too.

"I think that when you die you die. You become worm-meal, dust to dust, no rhyme, no reason, just dead."

Jack grinned. "Ah, spoken with the certainty of a man who has never died."

One of the stunning dignities of being human is the capacity to be certain and dogmatic about that which we know very little. Of this I am certain!

22

"If it's real, isn't it true?"

"Oh, not at all, Tony! And to make matters even more convoluted, something might be real but not actually exist at all, while truth remains independent from what is real or perceived to be real."

I am so guilty of this, creating false realities fabricated out of false perceptions based on false assumptions and then getting angry with people who tell me the truth. Or worse, I discount the nine things they were right about because they were wrong about one thing.

23 MARCH

"Honestly, I don't think I knew how to love her, or how to love anyone for that matter."

"Thank you, Anthony, for that admission. I am certain you are correct. But the point is that she believed in your love, and even though it didn't exist, it became so real to her that she built a world and life around it . . . twice."

So, if I don't know how to love, and I do my best to pretend that I do, is it still betrayal when it is exposed that I never did? Yes!

24

"So let's suppose this God is good all the time, never a liar, never a deceiver, always a truth-teller. One day this God comes to you and says this: 'Tony, nothing will ever separate you from my love, neither death nor life, not a messenger from heaven nor a monarch of earth, neither what happens today nor what may happen tomorrow, neither a power from on high nor a power from below, nor anything else in God's entire created cosmos; nothing has the power to separate you from my love.'"

I might smile, but I don't believe it!

25

"So, you listen to God tell you [of His love], but you don't believe it. Not believing it becomes what is real to you, and you then create a world that holds not believing the word of this God, or the love of this God, or even in this God at all, as a fundamental cornerstone of your life's construction. Here is one question nestled among many others: Does your inability to believe the word of this God make what this God has said not true?"

Yes! Wait . . . no! No! Really?

MARCH 26

"If you choose not to believe the word of this God, what would you 'experience' in relationship to this God?"

"Separation?" Jack filled in the blank. "Tony, you would experience a sense of separation, because separation is what you thought was 'real.' Real is what you believe, even if what you believe does not exist."

So . . . I am not powerful enough to change God's love for me? I can't behave my way into separation? Really . . . I mean, truthfully?

27 MARCH

"God tells you that separation is not true, that nothing can 'really' separate you from the love of God—not things, behaviors, experiences, or even death and hell, however you choose to imagine it; but you believe separation is real, and so you create your own reality based on a lie."

So, this sense of being separated . . .
that is a lie? And because I believe
the lie, it becomes "real" to me?
So I act and live as if I am separated
from that love? When I step away
into this lie, do you step closer?

28

"Then how does one ever know what is true? What is truth?"

The two greatest questions: The answer to the second is Jesus, who comes from outside my box, and the answer to the first is to ask him.

29 MARCH

"Standing at the fulcrum of history in the very presence and face-to-face with truth, [Pontius Pilate], as so many of us are wont to do, declared it nonexistent, or, to be more accurate, declared 'him' to be nonexistent. Thankfully, for all our sakes, Pilate did not have the power to turn something real into something that wasn't true." He paused before saying, "And, Tony, neither do you."

So, Jesus is the Truth! But I still have the power to not believe that, right?

30

"Tony, hell is believing and living in the real when it is not the truth. Potentially you could do that forever, but let me say something that is true, whether or not you choose to believe it, and whether or not it is real to you." He again waited. "Whatever you believe about death and hell, it is truly not separation."

This has to be True. Nothing else makes sense. Jesus, help me take sides with you against the way I see things.

31 MARCH

"Who am I? No, wait, where am I?" A man sat and cradled Tony in his arms, . . . and he relaxed into the man's embrace.

"Safe," the man whispered, and stroked his head. "You are safe, Tony."

So in all the effort I made to be safe, the truth is that I was safe the entire time, held inside Relentless Affection? I was safe from you even, though I wasn't safe from my own people.

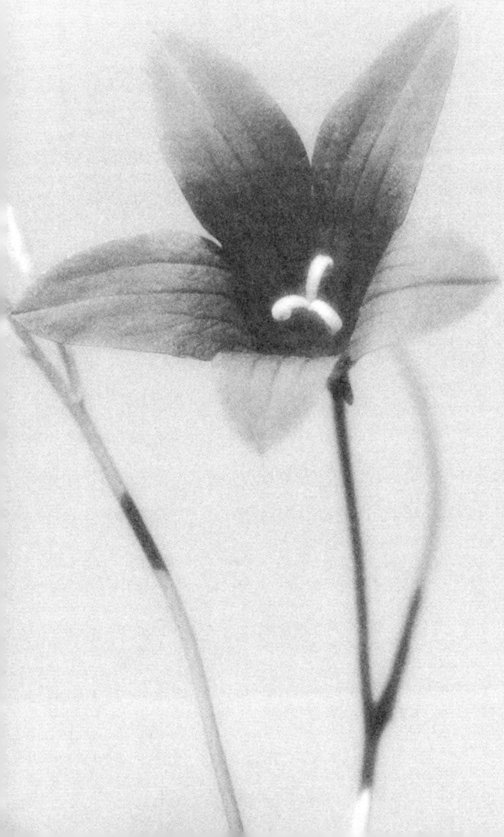

1 APRIL

The Month of Seeing

"It's time to rest a little. I am not leaving. I will always hold you, Tony."

"Who are you?"

I have always wanted to be held,
to have someone who wouldn't leave . . .
then I could rest. Who are you?

2

If the man answered, Tony didn't hear him as the night, like a blanket, wrapped him in a tender caress and he slept safely without dream or even wishful thought.

Tonight I would like to sleep, inside of your embrace, sound and without a care that robs my rest. Please?

3 APRIL

In general, the land looked worn and abused, spent. Thankfully, patches of mountain wildflowers and the occasional rose had populated some of the worst scars, as if softening a loss or grieving a death.

Probably something wrong with the soil, Tony surmised. It seemed water and sun were in supply, but so much depends on what lies beneath the surface.

So, what has to die in order that the soil of my heart begins to produce life instead of death? I'm not sure that I want to know the answer to that.

4

Something here called to him, or at least resonated. "Safe" had been the word this man had spoken over him. Not exactly a word he would have chosen.

I always thought that safe was alone, but I am beginning to understand that it is a word of trust, and trust involves an "other." Can we go back to performance? It might not be safe, but it certainly is easier than trust.

5 APRIL

"What is this place?" he asked.

"It's a habitation," the man responded, looking into the distance.

"A habitation? What exactly is a habitation?"

"A place to dwell, to abide, to be at home in, a habitation." The man said these words as if he loved this place.

How could you love a desolation?
What do you see that I don't?
Why would you ever want to live here?

6

They stood for a time, side by side, each seeing the place through different eyes—one compassionate, the other uneasy and a little dismayed.

How odd is this? Jesus sees us with compassion. We are uneasy with ourselves, if not disappointed.

7 APRIL

"But here," he said, his hand spanning the entire enclosure, "is the center, the heart of the habitation. What happens here changes everything."

There is a place in our inner worlds where everything about us comes together. Some day we will discover that this is exactly where Jesus pitched his tent.

8

"Who owns it?"

"No one. This place was never intended to be 'owned.'" He enunciated the last word as if it were slightly repulsive and didn't belong in his mouth. "It was intended to be free, open, unrestricted . . . never owned."

It is true: I don't want to be owned or even managed, but I am not eager to be independent either. Is there something in between, where I am free but connected? Relationship, perhaps?

9

He seemed to be one of those rare people who felt completely comfortable inside their own skin, and at peace with everything around him. There was no detectable agenda, no sense of someone looking for an advantage or angle like most everyone else he knew. Maybe content was the word, not that anyone in his or her right mind could ever be content out here in this loneliness.

I want to be a person comfortable inside my own skin, but I'm not, and I don't know how to get there. Please heal me.

"So tell me, if you would, who are you?" It was the obvious question.

The man deliberately turned to face him, and Tony found himself looking into those incredibly penetrating eyes. "Tony, I am the one your mother told you would never stop holding on to you."

Have I mentioned this trust issue? I would truly like to grow accustomed to your embrace, but this is not easy for me. Thank you for understanding.

11 APRIL

"Either I am who I say I am, or you believe deep down inside in a Jesus who would slap a person across the face. Which is it?"

I want you to do whatever it takes to shake me from the lies I believe. I would rather be free. I can't believe I am asking for this!

12

"Ha! Good for you! Dead people do bleed!" Jesus laughed and put his arm around Tony's shoulder. "At least you try and remain consistent with your assumptions, even when they aren't true and regardless of the difficulty they add to your life. Hard way to live, but understandable."

Why is it that I would rather hold on to my assumptions than take the risks to find out if they are false?

13 APRIL

"This place is only a shadow now of what it once was in its beginning. At one time it was all a wild and magnificent garden, open, lovely, and free."

Dear God, I don't want to be a shadow person. I want to be what I was intended to be. Please be the gardener of my heart.

14

"This, Tony, is a living land, not a construction site. This is real and breathing, not a fabrication that can be bullied into being. When you choose technique over relationship and process, when you try and shortcut the speed of growing awareness and force understanding and maturity before its time, this"—he pointed down and over the length and width of the property—"this is what you become."

I don't know another way to survive in this world. Please teach me so I might change.

15 APRIL

"Because you continue to inhabit and believe your metaphors, you cannot see what is true."

I have no memory of seeing, only of lies that I have told myself and what others have whispered and sometimes pounded into my soul. Touch my inside eyes that I might see!

16

"Are you telling me that all of this, and not just what I saw inside the walls but everything outside as well, all of this is a living being?"

The Jesus-man did not waver in his gaze. "I am telling you much more than that, Tony. I am telling you that this living being . . . is you!"

I have thought very little about the value and significance of who I am as a person, or about what my inside world looks like. Maybe I was afraid.

17

In an instant, his vision had changed, his eyes had opened, but now he desperately did not want to see through them. He had already judged this place from a superior position of aloof noninvolvement and declared it a no-man's-land of loss, a scrap heap not worth saving. That was his assessment.

Again I have become the judge and executioner, my deep shame the evidence against me, the prisoner who sees only self-loathing and hate in the eyes of the judge. I am doomed to the guilty verdict.

APRIL 18

Tony dropped to his knees and covered his eyes with his hands as if to conjure new lies to conceal the gaping emptiness left by the absence of the old ones, or secure a new delusion that might offer refuge, protection, and comfort. But once you "see," you can't "un-see."

I hated being blind, despised myself in my darkness, but there was a comfort to the imaginations I could create. "Seeing" is being apprehended by the true, and my hiding options have disappeared.

19 APRIL

Honesty compelled him to rip his hands from his face; clarity demanded a hearing. He looked again and this time looked deep. He found nothing he admired or felt affection toward. This place was a shattered waste, a complete and utter loss, a sad blemish in an otherwise potentially appealing world. Were this truly him, his own heart, he was a staggering disappointment, at best. At worst, he hated everything about himself.

I don't want to humble myself!

20

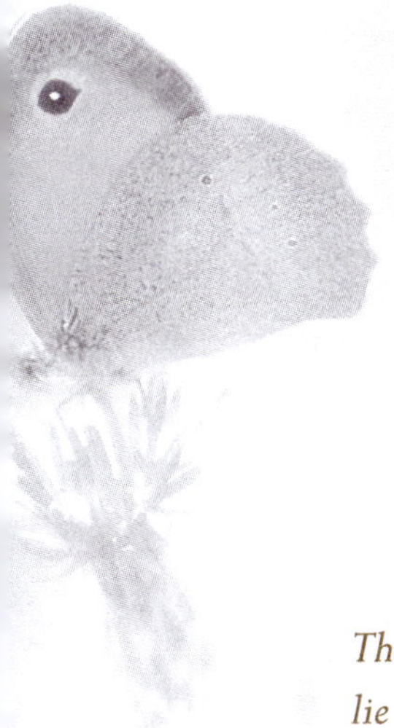

"Please, tell me it isn't true. Is this all I am, a sick and pitiful waste of a human being? Is this all my life is? Am I ugly and disgusting? Please, tell me it isn't true."

There is a liar in the soul, and the chief lie whispered to all is "I am not." I am not good enough, not special, not beautiful, not important, not enough. . . . Once I believed the lie, life became a slave's quest to find something that can prove "I am." Nothing else matters, really. It is a lie!

21 APRIL

Waves of self-pity and self-loathing pounded him until he felt the fabric of his soul was going to tear apart at its seams. A shock wave knocked him off his knees and slammed him to the ground. The Jesus-man knelt down and held him, letting him wail in his arms, strong enough to keep unbearable pain and loss inside a grasp of tender kindness. It felt as if the only thing holding him in one piece was the presence of this man.

I need someone to tell me who I am;
I know what I am not.

22

Caught in an emotional hurricane, Tony felt his mind tearing from its moorings; everything he had considered real and right was now turning to dust and ashes. But then, like a bolt of light, the opposite presented itself: What if he were actually finding his mind, his heart, his soul? He shut his eyes tight and sobbed, wanting to never open them again, to never again see the shame of what he was, what he had become.

There is a breaking of the heart, the soul, the mind, that is too deep for words.

23 APRIL

The Jesus-man understood and pressed Tony's weeping and snot-smeared face into his shoulder. As one wave of emotion would ease, a new upswelling would pummel him and he was washed away again, the pressure at times so intense he thought he was turning inside out. Surge after surge, years of buried emotions, waiting for jubilee, expressed, finally voiced.

Why does healing of the heart and soul
require that I "feel" what I have buried?
I suppose that it has been waiting.

24

"Every human being is a universe within themselves."

Human beings catch me by surprise,
and I see a depth beyond imagining . . .
and then I forget. Please help me remember!

25

"Your mother and father participated with God to create a soul who would never cease to exist. Your parents, as cocreators, supplied the stuff, genetics and more, uniquely combined to form a masterpiece, not flawless but still astounding; and we took from their hands what they brought to us, submitting to their timing and history and added what only we could bring to them—life. You were conceived, a living wonder who exploded into being, a universe within a multiverse, not isolated and disconnected, but entangled and designed for community, even as God is community."

My heart wants this to be true, but . . .

APRIL 26

"Ha! Living wonder?" Tony sniffled, limp from the exertion of fighting the flood. . . . "I'm not."

"For there to be an 'I am not,' there must first be an 'I am,'" Jesus encouraged. "Image and appearance tell you little. The inside is bigger than the outside when you have the eyes to see."

And I have spent a lifetime trying to decrease the inner to match my shame-based imagination of the outer. Did I tell you that I am blind?

27 APRIL

"I'm not sure I want to see, or know," mumbled Tony. "It hurts too much. Anyway, I don't believe any of this, including you, is real. And yet I still feel so ashamed. I would rather go back to my blindness, to not seeing."

Seeing, honesty, authenticity, integration . . . they all come with a cost. Not seeing, dishonesty, lack of integrity, disintegration . . . they all come with a cost.

28

"The hurt is real, and true. Trust me, Tony. Transformation without work and pain, without suffering, without a sense of loss is just an illusion of true change."

I so easily forget that the life I have been leading, protecting the lies in my life, has also been work and pain and suffering, without transformation.

29 APRIL

"I can't do this. And trust? That's not a word I've had in my vocabulary. Trust is not my thing."

"That's for sure," Jesus said and chuckled. "But it is my thing!"

Whew! It is a huge relief to know this is your thing and not mine. I'm always getting it wrong.

30

"Tony, your mother was the last person you trusted. You can't do any of this on your own or even on your own terms. You were created by a community to exist in community, made in the image of a God who has never known anything except community."

I know I am drawn toward relationship, but it is terrifying, too. Trust is terrifying. Can't you heal me without anyone else finding out about it?

1 MAY

The Month of Possibility

"God, a community?"

"Always. I told you I have never been alone. I've never done anything by myself. Relationship is at the very heart of who I am."

So why is it so hard for me to be open to relationships, if I am truly made in your image? Why would I often rather be lonely? Comfort, protection, pride, selfishness, fear?

2

"So, what happened to me? If this place is really me, how did I end up a lifeless and devastated wasteland?"

"From your point of view, you would say that 'life' happened to you: big and little losses inside the everyday; the accumulation and embracing of lies and betrayals; the absence of parents when you needed them; the failure of systems; the choices to protect yourself, which, while keeping you alive, also inhibited your ability to be open to the very things that would heal your heart."

Let me tell you what happened to me. . . . I am a story!

3

"And from your perspective?"

"From my perspective, it was death not life, an unreality you were never designed for. It was un-love, un-light, un-truth, un-freedom . . . It was death."

If I have identified "life" as the enemy, that "life" has treated me badly and unfairly, it would make sense that I would have little hope. Where would I turn, if away from life?

"Son, you have been dying since the day you were conceived. And even though death is a monstrous evil, human beings have imagined it into something much more powerful than it deserves, than it actually is, as if light were casting death's shadows in horrific proportions onto the backdrop of your existence and now you are terrified by even the shadow of death."

I have been told that these fleeting and fragile moments of time are all I have, that nothing else exists, a box that defines everything by its very walls . . . and I am terrified.

5 MAY

"For now, understand that a significant reason why you fear death is because of your atrophied and minuscule perception of life. The immensity and grandeur of life continually absorb and eradicate death's power and presence. You believe death is the end, an event causing a cessation of things that truly matter, and therefore it becomes the great wall, the inevitable inhibitor of joy, love, and relationship. You see death as the last word, the final separation."

I confess: I am a believer in death as final judge and executioner, as that which defines existence and meaning and purpose and destiny. Death has always been my master.

6

"The truth is," he continued, "death has only been a shadow of those things. What you call death is indeed a separation of sorts, but not anything like you imagine it. You have focused yourself and defined your existence with reference to the fear of that singular last-breath event rather than recognizing death's ubiquitous presence all around you—in your words, your touch, your choices, your sorrows, your unbelief, your lies, your judgment, your unforgiveness, your prejudices, your power-seeking, your betrayals, your hiding. The 'event' of death is only one small expression of that presence, but you have made that expression everything, not realizing that you swim in death's ocean every single day."

Help! I have always been drowning!

7 MAY

"Tony, you were not designed for death, but neither was death intended for this universe. Inherent in the event of death is a promise, a baptism in this ocean that rescues, not drowns. Human beings uncreated life and brought that un-life into your experience, so out of respect for you, we wove it from the beginning into the larger tapestry. You now experience this underlying tension between life and death every day until you are released through the event of death, but you were designed to deal with its encroachment in community, inside relationship, not in self-centered isolation like your little place here."

If this is true, it changes everything!

8

"When you don't deal with death, Tony, everyone in your world becomes either a catalyst for pain or dead to you. Sometimes it's easier to bury them somewhere on your property than to simply send them away."

It seems that we have made death the pornography of our modern world. We hide it, clothe it, mask it, dress it up, turn it into a ceremony, try to ignore it, but never face it. . . . I have not faced it!

9 MAY

"So death wins?" Tony knew what she was really asking, and if this Jesus-man was really . . . who he said he was, then he would know, too.

"Sometimes it feels like it, doesn't it? But no, life won! Life continues to win. I am living proof."

Death is everywhere, in the tragic accident just down the street, in the world numbing injustice of human trafficking, the ugliness of my own curt reply to a perceived offense. It rules both perpetrators and victims. Life won? When I am feeling death up close and personal, this truth sings to me, that You Are Life, enormously, unfathomably, and magnificently bigger!

10

"So you're not just a myth, then, a children's story? You really expect me to believe that you rose from the dead?" He wanted to hear him say it.

"Ha, it takes a lot more faith to believe that I didn't. That I was beaten unrecognizable, hung on the torture cross, speared through the side into the heart, buried dead in a tomb, and yet somehow resuscitated, unwrapped myself, rolled away a ton of rock, subdued the elite temple guard, and started a movement that is supposedly all about the truth of life and resurrection, but actually based on a lie? Yeah, much easier to believe."

I suppose we all have faith in something.

11

"Tony, I rose from the dead. We broke death's illusion of power and dominance. Papa God loved me to life in the power of the Spirit, and demonstrated that any ideology of separation would forever be insufficient."

If you rose from the dead, if you conquered death . . . then death is not the enemy I thought it was.

MAY 12

"What you are in the middle of at this moment, Tony, is called a crisis of faith. More often it happens in the moment of your physical death, the event, but since there have never been formulas governing relationships and you are not actually dead yet, something special and mysterious must be afoot."

Why does everything have to be a crisis?
I suppose that is what a cross roads really is,
an invitation to have my choices judged, in a
restorative way, special and indeed mysterious!

13 MAY

Tony was surprised. "Are you telling me that you don't know why I'm here?"

"No! Papa hasn't shared that piece of purpose with me so far." He leaned in as if to share a secret. "He knows I like surprises."

"Wait. I thought you were supposed to be God?"

"I'm not supposed to be God, I am God!"

"Then how come you don't know why I am here?"

"Like I said, because my Dad hasn't told me."

You like surprises! Jesus, will you teach my heart to look forward to surprise with excited expectancy instead of timid hesitation, tinged with a bit of dread?

14

"But if you are God, don't you know everything?"

"I do."

"But you just said you didn't—"

"Tony," Jesus interrupted, "you don't think in terms of relationship. You see everything through the grid of an isolated independence. There are answers to your questions that will absolutely bewilder you, make no sense whatsoever, because you don't even have a frame of reference that would allow them."

There is a relief in knowing that some things will always bewilder and remain mysterious.

15 MAY

"Part of the wonder of me, always God, joining the human race, is that I was not some actor added to the cast of characters, but literally became fully human as a forever reality. I never stopped being fully God, fully the creator. It is true now and has been since the beginning of time that the entire cosmos exists inside me and that I hold it all together, sustaining it, even now, right this moment, and that would include you along with every created thing. Death could never say that. Death holds nothing together."

I made death the center, a fear that holds nothing together. Why?

16

Jesus continued, "So, yes, I could draw upon my knowledge as God to know why you are here, but I am in relationship with my Father, and he hasn't told me, and I trust him to let me know if it becomes important for me to know. Until then, I will walk this out in real time and space with you, in faith and trust, and see what surprises Papa has in store for us."

Trust, there is that word again.
Can't you just give me something I can do?

17 MAY

"So let me get this right," Tony began. "There is Father, that's your Dad, and you would be the Son?"

"And the Holy Spirit," offered Jesus.

"So, who is the Holy Spirit?"

"God."

"This is a Christian thing, right? So you are telling me that anyone who believes in you believes in three gods? Christians are polytheists?"

I confess: It was a relief to find out Jesus was never a Christian.

18

"There are lots of folks besides Christians who believe in me. 'Believer' is an activity, not a category. Christians have only been around a couple thousand years. As for the question about them being polytheists? Not at all."

We all believe something, even if it is that life is meaningless, and whatever we believe we center our existence around. . . . So what do I actually believe?

19

"Listen carefully, Tony. There is only . . . hear me carefully: There is only one God. The darkness of the choice for independence has blinded humanity to the simplicity of the truth. So first things first—one God. As much as they disagree about the details, and the details and disagreements are significant and important; but the Jews with their sects, the Christians of every stripe and color, the Muslims with their internal diversity, all are in agreement about this: There is only one God, not two, not three, not more, just one."

Seems easy: one God.

MAY 20

"The Jews were the first to put it best in their Shema: 'Hear, O Israel: The Lord our God is one Lord!' But the Jewish Scriptures speak of this 'one' God as a plurality. 'Let "us" make Man in "our" image.' That was never intended as a contradiction about God being only one, but an expansion of what the nature of the 'one' was like. Rooted in the Jewish understanding was that essentially, and I use that word carefully, essentially the one was singular in essence and yet a plurality of persons, a community."

Not so easy:
a community of Persons.

21 MAY

Jesus raised his hand and Tony quieted.

"This is a gross oversimplification, but the Greeks, whom I love dearly, beginning especially with Plato and Aristotle, got the world consumed in thinking about the one God, but they didn't get the plurality part, so they opted for an indivisible singularity beyond all being and relationship, an unmoved mover, impersonal and unapproachable but at least good, whatever that meant."

How can we know what "good" really is? My definition put me at the center, and it hasn't turned out . . . good.

22

"And then I [Jesus] show up, in no way contradicting the Shema, but expanding on it. I declared in the simplest possible terms, 'The Father and I are one and we are good,' which is essentially a relational declaration. As you probably know, that solved everything, and finally the religious got their ideologies and doctrines straight and everyone agreed and lived happily . . ."

I confess: I enjoy it when you are even a little sarcastic. It gives me hope.

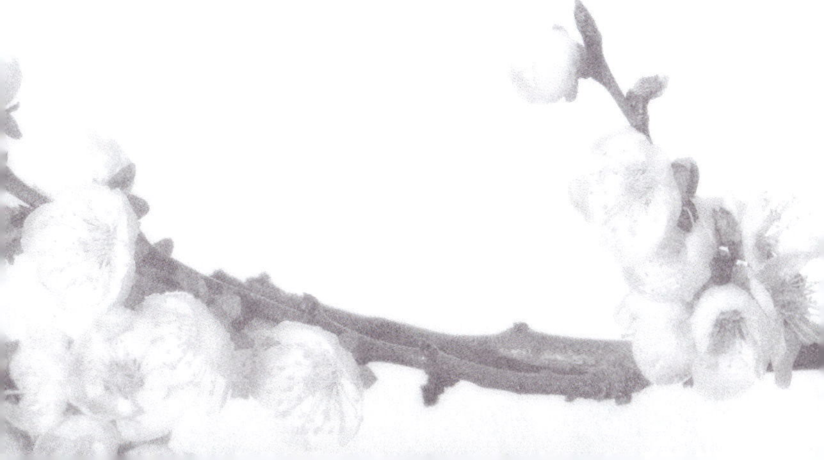

23 MAY

"To stay with my story, in the first few hundred years after my incarnation, there were many, like Irenaeus and Athanasius, who got it. They saw that God's very being is relational, three distinct persons who are so wonderfully close we are oneness. 'Oneness,' Tony, is different than an isolated and independent 'one,' and the difference is relationship, three persons distinctly together."

Distinctly . . . together? So "oneness" is not absorption, but celebration?

24

"The Greeks, with their love for isolation, influence Augustine and later Aquinas, to name only a couple, and a nonrelational religious Christianity is born. Along come the Reformers, like Luther and Calvin, who do their best to send the Greeks back outside the Holy of Holies, but they are barely in the grave before the Greeks are resuscitated and invited back to teach in their schools of religion. The tenacity of bad ideas is rather remarkable, don't you think?"

I confess: I have not only created bad ideas, but I found sick pleasure in the damage they caused. Is there forgiveness for me?

25 MAY

"Ah, all you need to know is this: At the heart of all existence is a great dance of self-giving, other-centered love—oneness. Nothing is deeper, simpler, and purer."

"I don't mind a little rain if it comes from above, or a little pain when it takes me to love. I can't say that I'm lost if I don't know what's found, but I know that I'm lost when you're not around." (DE)

26

So this desolate place was supposed to be his heart, if what he had been told could be believed. It was not exactly home, but not exactly hell either. The latter felt truer at the moment than the former.

I have become so comfortable inside the walls of my damage that I filled it with furnishings and called it my home. Now you want me to journey to a land that I do not know?

27

He cleared his throat. "Do you want . . ."

"Shhhh! Busy!"

He waited again until he couldn't help himself. "Uh, busy doing what?"

"Gardening. So many weeds."

Dear God, knowing that you are always there is sometimes irritating. Unlike my other "relationships," I can't seem to control you, and you rarely tell me what you are really up to.

MAY 28

"And what exactly am I doing here?"

"Agitating," she replied.
"Sit. Breathe in, breathe out, be still."

And so he sat, trying to be still on the outside, the rush of images, emotions, and questions rising like a slowly flooding river.

I confess: I have a difficult time being still and silent. I feel guilty, so I go and do something . . . anything, just so I don't have to be still and silent.

29 MAY

The woman, without opening her eyes and barely moving, reached over and put her hand on the bouncing knee and it slowed to a stop.

"Why you running so fast?"

What is it that I don't want to hear in the quiet? What would happen if I stopped running on the inside? Enough of that . . . gotta go!

30

"Anthony, why do you always think invitations are expectations?"

He grinned. He knew he didn't have to answer, that she already knew his thoughts. Invitations were expectations. There was always an agenda, sometimes obvious, often hidden, but always. Was there any other way to live in the world?

I know how to live in a world filled with agendas. To be loved without them . . . is very disconcerting.

31 MAY

"Praying? Who are you praying to?"

"I'm not praying to anyone," she replied, her eyes still closed. "I am praying with."

He tried to wait awhile, but it was not his habit. "So, who are you praying with?" he asked.

"With you!"

Not praying to, praying for, praying about . . . simply praying with? This is so simple and yet so hard, to stop being selfish in my relationship with you.

1 JUNE

The Month of Dismantling

Her eyes opened for the first time and he found himself looking again into those same incredible brown origins of light. He was looking at Jesus, but different. "Not Grandma," she observed, "Grandmother. Understand?"

I am learning, slowly, how easy you are to be with, how you wrap yourself in ways that I can understand, that you have a keen sense of humor from which all humor originates. I am liking this.

2

"You're going to forgive me something that I don't even understand?"

"Listen to me, dearest . . ." She paused, and Tony felt a wave of something painful and sweet in her use of that particular term of endearment. He let it wash over him, and as if she knew when it subsided, she waited before continuing, "Much of what you must forgive others for, and especially yourself, is the ignorance that damages. People don't only hurt willfully. More often because they simply don't know anything else; they don't know how to be anything else, anything better."

I don't know if I can. Help?

3

"May I come in?" he asked.

"Of course, you are always welcome here!" She warmly waved him inside.

Always?

JUNE 4

"You want to know why I live here, in this 'hovel'; I think that is the word you used, based on your civilized and educated perception?"

There was no use denying it. "Yes, I was wondering. So why?"

"It was the best you could give me."

Ouch! And yet, here you are, willing to go and be anywhere to love me.

5 JUNE

"It's all right, Anthony! I have no expectations. I am grateful to have found even this small place in your heart. I travel light"—she smiled as if at some secret thought—"and I make my home inside the simplest gifts. There is nothing to feel bad or ashamed about. I am thoroughly grateful, and being here is a joy!"

I confess: My "faith" is based on believing that your love is dependent upon my performance, and therefore "separation" is the word that defines how I think of you. I am a failure; you know that, right? Why would you want to be with me?

6

"So . . . because this is me, my world somehow, I have only made this small place for you? And for Jesus, I made a larger place, but it's still only a run-down ranch house . . . ?" He was suddenly saddened, and he wasn't sure why.

"It is his joy, too, to be here. He gladly accepted the invitation."

Perhaps the great discovery of faith is that Jesus has been inside us all the while, and he didn't come alone.

7 JUNE

"Invitation? I don't ever remember inviting him, or you for that matter. I'm not even sure who you are. I don't know if I ever knew enough to invite anyone."

Now she turned toward him, licking the spoon that she was using to stir the stew. "It wasn't your invitation, Anthony. If it had only been left up to you, we probably would never have had the opportunity to dwell here."

If it wasn't my invitation, being as blind and lost as I am, does that mean I also cannot get you to leave?

8

"The Father's invitation. Papa God."

"Jesus's Father . . . you mean, like God the Father?" Tony was surprised and upset. "Why would he invite you here?"

"Well, despite everything you believe about him or don't, and by the way, almost nothing you believe about him is true . . . regardless, Papa God cares for you with Relentless Affection. That is why we are here. We share in his affection."

I have always assumed that Jesus
liked me even if his Father did not. . . .
Maybe Jesus has a flaw in his character?

9 JUNE

Here was the catch, the hidden agenda, the reason all of this was dangerous and a lie. Whoever this woman was, and despite being drawn to her much as he was to Jesus, she had uncovered his fundamental assumption, the true heartache that he knew lived in the belly of his pain. If there was a God, he was a monster, an evil trickster who played with people's hearts, who ran experiments to see how much suffering human beings could endure, who toyed with their longings so they opened the beginnings of trust only to have everything precious destroyed.

I need you to reveal to me that all the ugly I believe about you is not true!

10

The fire highlighted her dignified presence and seemed to ignite an invisible perfume that wrapped the room in a sense of liturgy. It made no sense that Jesus and this woman were in any way related to the God they spoke about with such consideration.

Here is an ultimate conflict; if Jesus is only a human, is he of a different character than the one he calls his Father, and if he is God in our humanity, why do I not trust the one he calls his Father?

11

"So does this Father God live here . . . in my world?" he asked, a brittle edge on the words, thinking about the collection of lights at the bottom of the property.

"He doesn't, not as a habitation anyway. Anthony, you have never made a place for him, at least not inside these walls. While he is never absent, he also waits for you in the forest, outside the walls of your heart. He is not one who forces relationship. He is too respectful."

Forced love is no love at all. Controlling another is inherently disrespectful. Why do I believe the worst about God?

JUNE 12

Her demeanor was as gentle as a feather. He would have preferred hearing disappointment in her voice. That was manageable. Kindness was too slippery and intangible.

I have defenses against rage and disappointment, abuse and abandonment, but when I am confronted with kindness and love, the only defense I have is to run.

13 JUNE

"Always the businessman, Anthony. Joy and pleasure have value only if you can turn them into commodities? Nothing like damming a river and turning it into a swamp."

I have even prayed with self-serving, agenda-driven motives, and yet you see beyond to the longings and answer those. Thank you!

14

"Anthony, don't. I was making an observation, not a value statement. I don't expect you to be any different than you are. I know you, but I also know how you were forged and designed, and I intend to keep calling that from the deep, from the lost."

My shame has destroyed my ability to distinguish between an observation and a value statement. Do you understand that every statement of affection becomes another weight, an expectation, and an encroaching failure?

15 JUNE

"So, is that why I'm here, because I am dying? Does everyone go through this, whatever this is . . . this intervention? Is it to try and do what? Save my soul?"

I am asking this as an accusation and hoping that you know better, that I am asking this because my hope is almost gone and that you see beyond my words and into my desperation.

16

"If you guys are God, then why don't you do something? Why don't you just heal me? Why don't you send some church person up there and pray for me so that I don't die?"

I don't want relationship and the journey of trust that relationship requires. I want magic.

17 JUNE

"I am dying, and you are sitting here doing nothing. I may not be much, and I have obviously made a complete mess out of my life, but am I not worth anything to you? Am I not worth something? If for no other reason than that my mother loved me, and she was a good religious person, isn't that enough? Why am I here?"

The desperate . . . bargain. I will be furious if you refuse to play my game, but somewhere deep inside, I will be thankful.

18

"Why did you bring me here? So you could flaunt in my face what a worthless piece of crap I am?"

No one has ever had to convince me that I am a sinner, that I am damaged goods, that in my wounded responses I have hurt others. Your task is to help me understand that I am anything else.

19

Grandmother had not moved; she just watched him with those eyes. For the second time in less than hours he could feel another dam starting to collapse inside and with every ounce of strength he possessed, he tried to hold it back. It wasn't enough.

Can I tell you how I feel? Do you understand that I don't know how? I hate my own weakness, my inability to control this rising tide. I fear I might become unhinged. I also am afraid that I might never feel again.

JUNE 20

"What exactly do you want from me?
Do you want me to confess my sins?
Do you want me to invite Jesus into my life?
Seems a little late for that, don't you think?"

I have always assumed that my own salvation was ultimately dependent on something I could do.

21 JUNE

"Don't you realize how ashamed of myself I am? Don't you see? I hate myself. What am I supposed to think? Now what am I supposed to do? Don't you understand? I was hoping . . ." He broke down as a realization burst to the surface, sweeping over him. . . . "Don't you understand? I was hoping . . ." And then he said it, voiced the belief that had dominated his entire life, so deep that he was unaware of it even as he spoke it: "I was hoping . . . that death was the end."

What does that mean, that I have placed my hope in death and not in life?

22

"How else can I get away from what I've done? How can I escape myself? If what you're saying is true, I have no hope. Don't you see? If death is not the end, I have no hope!"

If death is not the end, all my choices have meaning; and if my choices have meaning, I am overwhelmed by what I then must face.

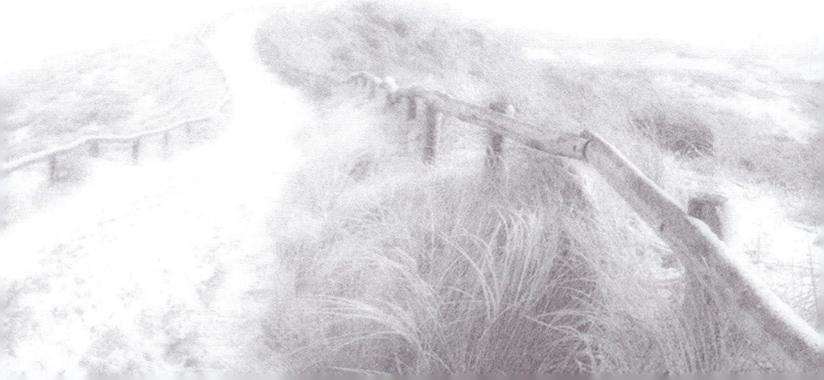

23 JUNE

"Oh, please, don't be sorry," reassured Jesus. "What you admitted to yourself was astounding! Don't minimize it because you are embarrassed. We think it was profound."

Why do you keep looking for the good in me? Even in my mess you keep calling to something deeper and substantial, as if it was actually there.

24

This should be good, he thought. *God having an idea.* Was that even possible? If you knew everything, how could you have an "idea"?

But then, how could God become fully human in Jesus? What does this say about the true nature of God, who would be so humble? What lies have I assumed?

25 JUNE

"Jesus, have I mentioned to you that you have . . ." He wanted to say "beautiful eyes," because it was what first came to mind, but concerned about being inappropriate he changed it to "remarkable eyes."

"Yeah, I get that a lot. Got them from my Dad."

Do I see, when I look at Jesus,
his Father's eyes?

26

"I've never liked your God Dad," admitted Tony.

"You don't know him," asserted Jesus, his voice unwavering, warm and kind.

"I don't want to know him," responded Tony.

"Too late, my brother," returned Jesus. "Like Father, like Son."

It changes everything to consider that to know Jesus is to know the Father.

27

Finally Tony asked, "Your Dad, isn't he the God of the Old Testament?"

It was Grandmother who responded, standing up and stretching. "Oh, the God of the Old Testament! He kinda freaks me out!"

Hah! Now this makes me laugh, but it does represent a real struggle I have. How do I resolve the character of Jesus with the caricatures of God as presented by my religious upbringing?

JUNE 28

"I don't understand."

Jesus smiled. "And that surprises you? Let me answer your question another way. That strong, courageous, and beautiful woman in there is the Holy Spirit."

I am beginning to believe that it is human and not a separating sin to not understand, to admit there is much that I do not know, and to be at peace with the unresolved.

29 JUNE

"Not exactly what I expected. I thought the Holy Spirit would be, you know, more ghostly, oozier or something, like a force field, not," he whispered, "some old woman." He lowered his voice till it was almost inaudible and mouthed the words, "who lives in a shack."

Especially when the "shack" is the place of our own inside house . . . who would believe that God would not only associate with such as I, but make a home here?

30

"I can do oozy. If you want oozy or ghostly, I can do that, too, and . . . if you don't think I like shacks, you don't know me very well."

The ease of their banter and relationship was entirely new to Tony. No underlying tension, no eggshells or minefields hidden in the conversations. He could not even detect agenda masked inside their words. It was real, authentic, compassionate, easy, enjoyable, and felt almost dangerous.

This is what my heart has longed for, to be in relationship that has no underlying tension. Could that even be a possibility?

1 JULY

The Month of Adventure

"Tony, you are about to go on a journey . . . on your 'journey,' it is important that you remember you will never be alone, no matter what it looks or feels like."

There is a "rest" even in the midst of activity and adventure, when you know that you are not alone in the deepest places, and you sense that your story is being woven into a larger tapestry, and your thread is essential because of the company you keep.

2

Again Jesus laughed, quietly and authentically, giving Tony the comfort that he was indeed fully present to him, fully there for him. "I am not about making you feel nervous; just wanted you to know that I will never stop holding on to you."

Does this mean that presence does not have to be controlling, and no matter my age, it is still possible and right to be the child?

3 JULY

With that she plopped down on the stool next to Tony, squirmed a little until she appeared comfortable while at the same moment producing from the folds of her garment what looked like several strands of light. He watched transfixed as she deftly brought various ends together, matching and connecting without thought or intention, but as light touched light their colors merged and transformations began.

A wonder of creativity expands the space I stand within, respecting my authority to hear for myself, in which I become larger and more true than I had before allowed, and calls me forward without a shred of shame.

4

Grandmother's arms opened wider to contain this treasure, and Tony witnessed the evolving of design that seemed impossible, as if his eyes could observe in ways his mind could not process. He was now experiencing the harmonies within his chest, from the inside, and the music seemed to grow as did the complexity of configurations. Hairline waves of brilliant color entangled with purpose and intent, each penetration creating a quantum participation, filaments of random certainty, chains of chaotic order.

Creation sings your name!

5

Suddenly Grandmother laughed like a little girl and gathered this grandeur inward until it was cupped in her hands. These she finally closed, until Tony could only see light pulsating through the spaces between her fingers. She brought it all slowly to her mouth as if to encourage embers, but instead blew like a cosmic magician, spreading her arms and opening her hands at the same moment to create a shape like a heart descending. The glory was gone.

Perhaps not gone, just visually imperceptible. What might this glory be? It is pure goodness!

JULY 6

"So, what I just saw, that . . . whatever that was that you just did, did you just make that up as you went, or was that the design of something specific?"

"That is a brilliant question, Anthony. What you saw, heard, and felt is a very tiny presentation of something very specific."

"And what is that, specifically?" Tony was eager to know.

"Love! Self-giving, other-centered love!"

God was "other" before there was creation, before rebellion, before independence. The "other" was this love. We have another word for "other"; it is "Holy"!

7 JULY

"One more thing, Anthony. You couldn't have noticed, but there was something essential purposefully left out of my little composition. You heard and felt the harmonies of light, at least the surface of them, but you didn't notice, did you, that the melody was missing?"

How could all the harmonies of creation exist without a melody?

8

"I don't understand. What's the missing melody?" he asked.

"You, Anthony! You are the melody! You are the reason for the existence of what you witnessed and consider so immeasurably awe inspiring. Without you, what you perceived would have no meaning and no shape. Without you, it would have simply . . . fallen apart."

This is the thought too deep for words in any language . . . that "you," dear reader, are the melody!

"It's okay, Anthony. I know you don't believe much of this yet. You are lost and looking up from a very deep hole just to see the superficial. This is not a test you can fail. Love will never condemn you for being lost, but love will not let you stay there alone, even though it will never force you to come out of your hiding places."

How could you be so "other" than everything I thought I knew and all that I believed experience had taught me?

10

"Anthony, I am she who is more than you can begin to imagine and yet anchors your deepest longings. I am she whose love for you, you are not powerful enough to change, and I am she whom you can trust. I am the voice in the wind, the smile in the moon, the refreshing of the life that is water."

There must be a source of all this yearning;
the underlying beauty, quality, and elegance
that leave me interfered by wonder and
hungry for something other.

11 JULY

"I am the common wind that catches you by surprise and your very breath. I am a fire and fury opposed to everything that you believe that is not the Truth, that is hurting you and keeping you from being free. I am the Weaver, you are a favorite color, and he"—she tilted her head toward Jesus—"he is the tapestry."

. . . and you are an essential thread in the tapestry, a favorite color. This is a mystery, an inclusion, and a belonging beyond my comprehension.

12

Jesus reached over and took Tony's hand. "The gift I spoke of earlier, Tony, is that on this journey you are taking, you can choose to physically heal one person, but only one, and when you choose the one, your journey will end."

I suppose the whole point of an adventure is the unexpected.
If I live without expectations,
would all of life be an adventure?

13

Jesus leaned closer. "You can't actually heal anyone, not alone, but I will be with you, and anyone you choose to pray for, I will heal through you."

I suppose this means that healing is relational, not magic?

JULY 14

"Good! So lemme ask you, do I have to believe for this to work?" He again looked back at the fire, bare remnants remaining, yet heat emanating from it strong and certain. He wasn't certain he heard the answer, but thought later that Jesus had replied, "Healing isn't about you, Tony."

I lived so much of my life as if everything was about me. I need help in changing that. Does that make it still about me?

15 JULY

Molly Perkins was angry and tired. The life of a single mom was routinely difficult, but on days like today seemed impossible. God wasn't supposed to give you more than you could handle, but she felt at the last-straw point of the load. Did God include the baggage that she herself had added to the weight of what she was supposed to handle? Did God take into account what others brought and dumped on her? She hoped so.

Today has been too much. I felt at the brink of everything coming undone, and then this! I am learning you are not a fixer or formula, but I do need to know that you will stay here with me in this difficult place.

16

Compassionate people, like the doctor Molly was verbally castigating, were among the dedicated many in the trenches, and while these might later weep their losses into pillows in secure homes, on duty they held it together. They, too, knew the haunting guilt of continuing to live, laugh, play, and love while others, often young and innocent, slipped from their best attempts at rescue.

I want to thank you for all of the people who inhabit the in-betweens, spending their hearts on standing with us as our worlds fall apart. Please bless them!

17 JULY

Some men, when confronted by their own mortality or the embarrassment, unwanted attention, and intrusion brought into their lives by a child beneath their expectations, justify their cowardice with noble language and slip out the back door.

Why is it we men are usually the ones who run from relationships, from consequences, from the hard choices? Why do we think our independence will lead to a better life than doing the work?

18

The arrival of the unforeseen reveals the depths of one's heart. A small ambiguity, the exposure of a tiny lie, an extra bit of the twenty-first chromosome, the replacement of the imagination or ideal by the real, almost anything unexpected can cause life's wheels to lock up and the facade of control to reveal its inherent arrogance.

There is so much that I cannot control,
and yet I act with the arrogance that
all of life is contained inside my power.
I am a fool! Please forgive me!

19 JULY

Thankfully, most women do not see escape as the option that some men do, and Molly responded to her losses by pouring her heart and soul into her son.

I am so grateful for women who do not run, who embrace the work and its costs and their children! Without the woman there would be no salvation, no seed "of the woman," which brought salvation to us all.

20

It was not only that he was seeing through his eyes; he could feel the emotions tumbling through the boy's inside world, his soul, and everything screamed trust regarding this woman.

> *I am uneasy when my instincts for survival conflict with the presence of a person who slips past my borders. Can you see? I have one hand up declaring "Halt!" but my other hand is waving you in.*

21

His opinions on most nonbusiness matters may not have been founded on evidence or experience, but he was sure of them. People like Cabby were an unproductive drain on the resources of society; they were valuable only to their families. He believed they were tolerated because of liberal persuasions, not because such people had any intrinsic worth. Tony could recall himself spouting such views at cocktail parties without the slightest stab of conscience. It is easy to create a category of persons, like retarded or handicapped, and then pass judgment on the group as a whole. He wondered if that was not the heart of all prejudice. It was so much easier than considering each as an individual, loved and loving.

I hate categories, but they are essential if I need to judge others.

JULY 22

And then she leaned down and laid her head on Cabby's chest and began singing something that Tony hadn't heard since . . . when? Not since he was a little boy. Now in this woman's voice he could hear his own mother's song, and suddenly he was deeply sad. He felt tears sliding down his face as this mother sang, "Jesus loves me, this I know."

Why does this simple statement find resonance in the deep and hidden? It sings to a profound longing.

23 JULY

"So, why was I there, and why am I back?"

"There are lots of reasons why you are there," she began. "Papa never does anything for just one purpose, and most of these you will never understand or even know. All part of the weaving."

I'm clinging to this thought that nothing is devoid of the possibility of purpose. Will you help be my trust that this is True, that I don't have to understand and control for you to be working in this?

24

"So will you tell me one of the reasons?" he asked.

"One reason, dearest, was to hear your mother sing to you. If nothing else, that was enough."

Does a mother's song mirror an eternal harmony sung from creation's beginnings—this love of a parent for a child, that is reason enough to exist?

25 JULY

"Trying to explain a human being," she began, "a being who is a unity, one, and yet comprising spirit, soul, and body, is like trying to explain God: Spirit, Father, and Son. The understanding is in the experience and relationship."

I am so used to thinking with only my head, of everything bowing to my mind. Please teach me another way.

26

"Cabby, like you, is a spirit interpenetrating a soul interpenetrating a body. But it is not simply interpenetration. It is dance and participation."

The dance of Person and Relationship allows for the possibility of participation. "Participation" assumes that I matter!

27 JULY

"Cabby's body is broken and his soul is crushed and bent, yet his spirit is alive and well. But even though alive and well, his spirit is submitted in relationship to the broken and crushed parts of his person, his soul and body. Words are very inadequate to communicate sometimes. When I tell you 'his body' or 'his soul' or 'his spirit,' it sounds like each is some thing or piece that you own. It is more accurate if you comprehend that you 'are' your body, and you 'are' your soul, and you 'are' your spirit. You are an interpenetrated and interpenetrating whole, a unity of diversity but essentially a oneness."

I have such little respect for the human creation. Please open my understanding.

28

"Yeah, don't go feelin' bad for him. His brokenness is just more obvious than yours. He wears it on the outside for all to see, while you have kept yours all locked away and hidden as best you know how. Cabby has internal sensitivities and receptors that are significantly more developed than yours. He can see things that you are blind to, can pick up on the good and the danger in people quicker than you, and his perception is much keener. It is just housed in an inability to communicate, a broken body and soul reflective of a broken world."

Why do I feel superior to the "obviously broken"? Why does it make me feel better about my hidden damage?

29

"Now don't you go all comparin' yourself and feelin' bad," Grandmother continued. "You and Cabby are on different journeys because you are each uniquely your own person. Life was never meant to be about comparing or competing."

Compare, compete, contrast—all expressions of the need to control . . . which is the only world I know. Is there another way to "be"?

JULY 30

"So, then, what is a soul, exactly?" he queried.

"Ah, now there is a deep question. To which there is no exact answer. Like I said, it is not a possession, it is a living. It is the Cabby-who-remembers, it is the Cabby-who-imagines, it is the Cabby-who-creates, who dreams, who emotes, who wills, who loves, who thinks. But Cabby as soul is housed inside the dimensions limited by who Cabby is as a damaged body."

I don't know how to think holistically about myself or anyone else. I want to be whole. Is that akin to being holy?

31 JULY

"Fair?" Grandmother mumbled. "That's a good one. Anthony, there is nothin' fair in a broken world full of broken people. Justice tries to be fair, but fails at every turn. There is never anything fair about grace or forgiveness. Punishment never restores fair. Confession doesn't make things fair. Life is not about granting the fair reward for the right performance. Contracts, lawyers, disease, power, none of these care about fair. Better to take dead words out of your languages, maybe focus on living words like mercy and kindness and forgiveness and grace. You might stop being so concerned about your rights and what you think is fair."

When "fair" matters less, I grumble less. When I complain less, suddenly I find room for thankfulness.

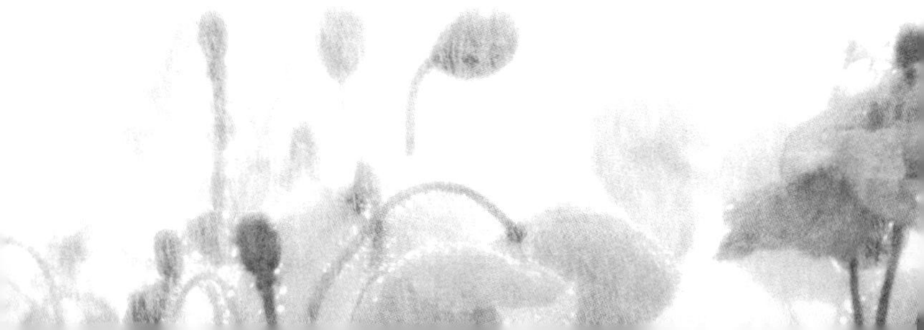

1 AUGUST

The Month of Deepening

"So why don't you fix him?" Tony asked quietly.

Grandmother was equally soft in her response. "Anthony, Cabby is not a broken toy, a thing to be fixed. He is not a piece of property to be renovated. He is a human being, a living being who will forever exist."

I don't like being around obvious hurt. I want it fixed now, resolved! Why am I self-conscious in the presence of disability? Am I reminded?

2

"Anthony, you barely know anything about this man, only what you assume from a snippet of a conversation. Where you think scumbag, I think lost sheep, lost coin, lost son, or"—she nodded toward him—"lost grandson."

I so easily forget that
I'm not that much less lost.

3 AUGUST

She let him sit inside his own judgment, wrestling with the implications of how he looked at everything, and everyone. It made him feel sick inside. He was internally facing another massive darkness that he had long treasured, and it grew as he rationally scrambled to justify himself. No matter the mental gymnastics or how he tried to mask it, his first inclination to pass judgment emerged more hideous and terrifying, a threat that might destroy anything within him that could ever have been considered good.

The ocean of shame has no bottom.

"This is not a time for self-loathing, Anthony," she said gently. "It is important that you realize you needed the skill to judge in order to survive as a child. It helped keep you and your brother safe. You and he are alive today partly because the ability to judge was in your toolbox. However, such tools eventually become debilitating and damaging."

What were these gifts intended for, these abilities that emerge in children when they are forced to find a way to survive?

5

"But I saw it. It's so ugly. How do I stop?" He was almost begging.

"You will, dearest, when you trust something else more."

Thank you for not tearing out of my grasp the very things that kept me alive, for not being disappointed in me or ashamed of me.

AUGUST 6

The dark wave had receded, but he knew it wasn't gone, just a monster in waiting, lurking for another opportunity. For the moment it was tamed by the presence of this woman. This was no longer only a game or lighthearted adventure. This was war, and it seemed that the battlefield was in his own heart and mind; something old and hurt was in conflict with something that was beginning to emerge.

I don't often treat my healing with the serious respect it deserves, as if this territory had no true value.

7 AUGUST

Then came the next unexpected; looking back into the mirror, Cabby asked in a halting attempt to form the words, "Tah-Ny lob Cnabby?"

Tony was caught, suddenly trapped by the three-word question. Cabby made the effort and had the will to ask, but Tony didn't have what it took to answer. Did he love Cabby? He didn't really know him. Did he know how to love anyone? Had he ever known what love was? And if he didn't, how would he recognize it if he ever found it?

I suppose I cannot truly love
until I truly know I am loved.

8

Tony was unaccustomed and captive to this world, but felt a grounding reality in each experience. This was life, ordinary yet extraordinary and unexpected. Where had he been all these years? Hiding was the answer that came to mind. It might not be the whole truth of it, but it certainly was a part.

Touch my eyes that I might see how everything is holy, that beneath the seeming ordinary lies the extraordinary.

9 AUGUST

Spending time with these children was both unexpected delight and difficult, his failures as a parent painfully obvious. He had tried diligently for a time, even read books on fathering and given it his best business try, but after Gabriel . . . he had left such matters to Loree and returned to the safer world of performance and production and property. Any pang of regret that surfaced throughout the day, he would push back into the closets and corners of his soul where they could be better ignored.

Why is it that in relationship with children, clarity emerges?

10

He smiled to himself, remembering how he and Jake had schemed together and "gone forward" one night at church, thinking it would win them points with the family, which it did. The attention their conversions garnered was initially rewarding, but it soon became clear that "asking Jesus into your heart" dramatically increased expectations for strict obedience to a host of rules they hadn't anticipated. He soon became a "backslider," in a category, he discovered, that was profoundly worse than being pagan in the first place. It was difficult enough surviving as a foster child. A foster child who had fallen from grace was magnitudes worse.

Why would there be greater respect afforded me as an "ungodly pagan," a proper target for religious marketing, than to be a "believer" who is less than perfect?

11 AUGUST

Tony was impressed at the blend of race and age, the financially secure rubbing shoulders with the less so. The ease of interactions was surprising, as was the general sense of kindness and community. This was different than he remembered.

There is a stunning beauty to the "Church," as community, diverse and open, respectful of the uniqueness of the journey that each is on, and kind in her compassion. We want more of that please, Holy Spirit!

12

This young man somehow knew that a sweetness lay outside his power to have or hold, and he was sharing this longing with him. Cabby would never experience a gift that Tony had treated with callous disdain—the love of a girl. Cabby treasured what he had handled with reckless contempt. Again Tony realized how shallow were his assumptions regarding the maturity of this sixteen-year-old's heart. It was not a painful, shaming self-judgment, but an exposure and uncomfortable. It seemed Tony was growing a conscience, and he wasn't sure he wanted one.

Teach me how to embrace the losses that in this life I will never recover. I know if I continue to focus on what I have not, I will lose sight of what I have been given.

13

The childlike wonder and simple colors—bright reds and greens and blues—of Cabby's soul had been exchanged for an older, more crafted environment, with deep textures and patterns, complexity, along with a breadth of space and maturity.

> *There is a fineness to aging, an intensifying and increasing. It takes time and attention to recognize its persevering quality, and it can take your breath away.*

AUGUST 14

Someone had once told him that the eyes were the windows of the soul, and maybe it was true; perhaps they actually were.

The eyes are portals into expanding universes. The action is in the eyes, and if the eyes are darkened, the other senses rise to open other doors.

15 AUGUST

"We just need to keep trustin' that God is right here, in the middle of the mess."

"I'm trying, Maggie, but some days just seem so much harder than other days, and some days I start to think that God is off doing more important things for more important people, or that I've done something wrong and he's punishing me, or . . ."

Is everyone important to you?
Help me to understand your very presence
as you being active and involved.

16

"I don't even know what to pray anymore," Molly stammered between her sobs. "I go up there, and in room after room, there are fathers and mothers who are just waiting, waiting to smile again, waiting to laugh, waiting to live. We are all just holding our breaths, waiting for a miracle. And I feel so selfish, praying that God would heal my baby, that somehow I could get his attention or if he would just tell me what I needed to do, and everyone else is praying, too, for their babies, and I don't get it and it's too hard."

Do you feel what I feel, or do you feel it deeper? Some days are almost too hard to bear, when grace is something I am holding on to in one-minute increments. Please "be" with me!

17 AUGUST

Maggie said nothing. She just held her friend, stroking her hair and handing her tissues. Sometimes silence speaks loudest and presence brings the most comfort.

I am not asking you to speak into the pain that now I feel, or answer all my questions that will give me eyes to see. Would you simply stay here with me and maybe gently catch my tears. You see, I'm finding in your silent touch a voice that I can hear.

18

He had a bigger and more important plan for his one opportunity to heal, and it didn't include Lindsay. It even made him a little angry that God would manipulate him like this, putting him in the middle of a situation that might tempt him to deviate from that purpose.

I confess: It seems that as I become more whole, my sensitivity is heightened about smaller degrees of my own stupidity. That makes me angry at times . . . just sayin'!

19 AUGUST

"Hmmm," mumbled Maggie, not convinced. "So why are you here, in our worlds?"

"I really don't know," he answered, which was mostly true. "I suppose we will have to trust God with that." In his mouth his words sounded plastic and fake, and he winced, but it was an easy way to avoid the question.

We liars become so adept at crafting words to answer without telling the truth. It is a skill I don't want, but don't know how to let go. Help!

20

"Maggie 'happened' to be there and helped me clean up. She couldn't stop laughing and turned a mess into a new possibility. She was an answer to prayer, and that's what Maggie is. God's kiss of grace."

A Kiss of Grace and the Kingdom of God seem to me to be one and the same. Thank you!

21

Maggie smiled. "I would say the same thing about Molly and the kids. After my 'history,' home is not as much about a place you belong as people you belong to. I belong here." Tony knew it was true. He could feel it as she spoke, and he suddenly felt lonely.

I have never found a place that I belonged, but you have given me to people to whom I now belong. Among all the gifts you have graced me with, these are the best!

AUGUST 22

"This moment contains all moments anyway, no need to be anywhere other than now."

"You are caught, as it were, in between life-before and life-after, and the bridge that is connecting the two is inner-life, the life of your own soul."

This is where I want to be alive, in the moment, in this one day's worth of grace. This is real, and you live here with me, not in some fear-based imagination.

23 AUGUST

"So this afterlife, I mean, this life-after, what is it like?"

". . . You are asking me something where the knowing is in the experiencing. What words exist that truly communicate the sensations of a first love, or an unexpected sunset; the smell of jasmine, gardenia, or oriental lilac; or the first time a mother holds her baby; or the moments you are surprised by joy; or a piece of music that is transcendent; or standing for the first time on a mountain you have conquered; or a first taste of honey from the comb . . . Throughout history we have been searching for words that link what we know to what we long for, and all we get are glimpses through a glass darkly."

I confess: I need a new prescription for my glasses!

24

"*T*his root is the life-before, everything you know and experience rippled as it is with foretastes of something else, something more. And within what you know and experience, all part of the root, you find hints of the flower—in music and art and story and family and laughter and discovery and innovation and work and presence. But having seen the root only, could you begin to imagine such a wonder as the flower? There will be a moment, Tony, when you finally see the flower, and in that moment everything about the root will make utter and complete sense. That moment is the life-after."

I see the root. Please help me
trust that there is a flower.

25 AUGUST

Again he wondered, *Where have I been all these years?* He had never really lived, as far as he could remember. But along with that thought came others, small remembrances of mystery that had penetrated his rush and agenda, bits of light and love and wonder and moments of joy that had whispered to him in his pleasures but screamed for attention in his pain. He had never been one to sit, to listen, to look, to see, to breathe, to wonder . . . and it had cost him, of that he was now certain. He felt, in this moment, like a waste, expressed in the damage of the land outside this window.

So, that penetrating whisper of mystery . . .
that was you?

26

"Tony, you are a root," Jack said, interrupting his spiral, "and only God knows what the flower will be. Don't get lost castigating yourself for being a root. Without the root, the flower can never be. The flower is an expression of what now appears so lowly and unimportant, a waste."

"It's the melody," exclaimed Tony, finally understanding, even if only a little.

Now this is a mystery, but true and worthy of full acceptance, that you, dear reader, are the melody at the very center and heart of God's harmony! Really!

27 AUGUST

"The way you see me right now, Anthony, is the best that your recollections can conjure up, a composite of memory and imagination of how your mind thinks I should look to you. You are a root looking at a root."

"I see men, but they look like trees walking." I need more healing.

28

"And if I saw you in the life-after?"

"Well, this might sound like sheer self-aggrandizement to you, but it would be true for anyone you encountered in the life-after. If from where you sit now you saw me as I truly am, you would probably fall on your face in reverence and worship. The root would see the flower and it would undo you."

I knew it! Somewhere deep inside I knew there was "more"—an intention and destiny that will one day swallow up all the losses.

29

"In life-after, I am everything that I was intended to be, more human than I ever succeeded in being on earth, and fully dwelt within by everything God is. You have barely heard one note of a symphony, seen one color of a sunset, heard one drop of a waterfall. You are rooted in your life and grasping after anything that will bring you a sense of transcendence, even turning other roots into the imagination of flowers."

Will you please help me apprehend that this life is not only about me?

AUGUST 30

"Jack," he confessed, "my life that I defined as a success is actually a total shambles, and yet you're suggesting that underneath it all, there is an unimaginable beauty? Are you telling me that I matter? That even though I am this ugly, ordinary-looking root, that I was designed and intended to express a unique and extraordinary flower?"

My heart sings, though hesitantly, that this is true, and I can hear in my breath a sigh of relief. I now can see another, and myself, with an open heart instead of judgment.

31 AUGUST

"And I assume," Tony continued, "this is true about every human being, each person born—"

"Conceived!" interrupted Jack.

"Each person 'conceived' on the planet, each one living in life-before, each one is a root in which a flower is waiting? Right?"

The question then remains: Would I be opposed to believing in a God who is of such magnificence and magnitude of love that every human being was the melody and center of their Relentless Affection?

1 SEPTEMBER

The Month of Confrontation

"So why all the crap, Jack? Why all the pain and disease and war and loss and hate and unforgiveness and cruelty and brutality and ignorance and stupidity and . . ." The litany of evils came spewing out, a list terrible in their speaking. "You know what we do with roots, Jack. We burn them, we use and abuse them, we destroy them, we sell them, we treat them like the disgusting pieces of detritus we think we are ourselves!"

There is this problem of evil, in ourselves and in creation, that we struggle with so deeply, especially in the light of your character as good and powerful.

2

"The problem of pain," he said softly, "is a root issue."

And so it is! Knowing what we would do with our freedom, why did you choose to go ahead with it anyway?

3 SEPTEMBER

"I don't know, Jack," he revealed. "I don't know if I can face all my stuff. The pile is awful and high."

"No worries, dear boy," responded Jack kindly. "You will cross that road when you come to it. You must remember, Tony, that there is not one good thing, or memory, or act of kindness, not one thing that is true and noble and right and just, that will be lost."

If you are indeed the "Good," and all that is good originates in you, and you are eternal in nature, then I can begin to understand how the good can never be lost. Deep breath!

"Somehow the pain, the losses, the hurt, the bad, God is able to transform these into something they could have never been, icons and monuments of grace and love. It is the deep mystery how wounds and scars can become precious, or a ravaging and terrifying cross the essential symbol of Relentless Affection."

The cross! We (humans) invent a device of monstrous torture, and embracing it, God transforms the cross into a symbol, icon, and monument of grace!

5

"Is it worth it?" whispered Tony.

"Wrong question, son. There is no 'it.' The question is and has always been, 'Are you worth it?' and the answer is and always, 'Yes!'"

Even the salvation of the entire cosmos does not justify the cross!

SEPTEMBER 6

"Jack, is this place, this in-between place that I know somehow is me . . . Was I brought here to be confronted with what I have done wrong?"

"No, my dear boy, quite the reverse," Jack assured. "The in-between and the life-after is centered and built upon everything you got right, not what you got wrong. And it's not that what you got wrong is inconsequential or just disappears; much of it is all around you as you can see, but the focus is on the rebuilding, not on the tearing down."

Sometimes I feel like I am entirely a wasteland, but then I sense you digging in the rubble and finding something with which you can build. Thank you!

7 SEPTEMBER

"Yes, the old must be torn down for the new to be raised; to have a resurrection you must have a crucifixion, but God wastes nothing, not even the wrong we have imagined into existence. In every building torn down there is much that remains that was once true and right and good, and that gets woven into the new; in fact, the new could not be what it is without the old. It is the refurbishing of the soul."

In the heaving anguish of my soul I declare, "Whatever you have built IN me, it is good and only good!" (September 7 is Cabby's [Nathan V's] birthday.)

8

"We are masters at building up facades, only to tear them down ourselves. In our independence we are very destructive creatures, first creating houses of cards and then knocking them down with our own hands. Addiction of every imagined sort, the will to power, the security of lies, the need for notoriety, the grasping of reputation, the trading in human souls . . . all houses of cards that we try and keep together by holding our breath. But, thanks to the grace of God, we must someday breathe, and when we do, the breath of God joins ours and everything collapses."

Breathe in me deep . . .
that I might breathe . . . and live!

"I do, sir, believe that the Holy Spirit leads us into truth, but sometimes we can't see the building for the underbrush, and sometimes it takes time for our eyes to heal."

I suppose the bear in the zoo doesn't care about what color the bucket is that holds his food.

10

Skor was flustered in the presence of a man undeterred, and as often happens when someone is caught inside their own assumptions, he changed the argument to something more personal. "You, young man, are contradicting centuries of church history, of theological minds much smarter and wiser than either of ours, and they agree with me."

Are you suggesting that to question my religious heritage is not an affront to you? You don't take it personally?

11 SEPTEMBER

"I'm so sorry, Maggie," he apologized. "I don't think Horace is a bad man, he just doesn't know any better. I had no idea what was coming down, and I'm embarrassed that I was any part of it."

Job and position security (fear) profoundly impacts interpretation of Scripture. We all bring what we have.

12

Tony was now in no mood to meet anyone, especially neighbors. He was caught in the immediate turmoil and upheaval of his inner world. Listening to Maggie's conversation with Jake had dismantled him, filling him with more self-loathing and tapping into a rush of uncomfortable memories he'd concealed inside well-constructed internal compartments. He didn't understand why, but he felt his guard collapsing. He could no longer stuff his feelings into private vaults and bury them.

Change is unsettling and often painful, especially when it catches me by surprise.

13

As they approached, Tony felt deep and increasing isolation and loneliness, as if their impending presence was pushing him into a corner. Strangely, the duo, who appeared huge at a distance, seemed to diminish in stature as they advanced.

There are certain enemies who look larger at a distance. Fear has a way of expanding our imaginations.

"That's a flower!" exclaimed Tony.

Sam looked at it carefully before turning back. "No, it's not! It's a weed. See, it has color, so it's a weed. And it's covered in all these nasty, prickly . . . uh . . ."

"Thorns," offered Bill.

"Yes, that's it, thorns. Why would a flower have a thorn? This is a weed! And we pull them and burn them so they don't spread. That's what we do, and we are very skilled at it, we are."

Our Enemy would try to convince us that the flowers in our lives are weeds.

15 SEPTEMBER

"Others?" asked Tony. "How many of you are there?"

"Hundreds!" responded Bill immediately. He looked up at Sam, perhaps for permission or support, but getting neither, continued, "All right, thousands; there are thousands of us." He paused as if thinking. "To be honest, there are millions of us, pulling weeds and keeping the walls 'cause that is what we do . . . keep walls, millions and millions of us, weed pulling, wall-keepers."

Liars take on the power you give them,
expanding into the space you give them.

16

"Keep away from you?" retorted Tony. "I want to meet your benefactors."

"Oh, that is not possible," sputtered Bill, shaking his head.

"And why not?"

"Because . . . you'll explode, that's why not, into millions and millions of pieces. Little tiny bits of bone and flesh and disgusting stuff flying in a million directions . . . not pretty, well, maybe mildly pretty in a repulsive sort of way."

Lies will often approach as friends, deflecting attention from them until you believe they act in your best interest.

17 SEPTEMBER

"But you named us, or rather, we were named after your behaviors and choices? We belong to you. We, you see, are your Bluster and your Swagger."

"It is true, Tony," came the voice of Grandmother, who had suddenly appeared next to him. "They are here because you gave them a voice and a place in your soul. You thought you needed them to become successful."

Lies will act as the good, convincing you that protection from consequences is the same as keeping you safe. That is a lie.

18

"I owe you?" asked Tony, distraught at what he now realized. "What was winning, especially if I had to use Bluster and Swagger to succeed? If you exist because I thought I needed you, I am a greater fool than both of you put together. I didn't need you, I needed honesty and integrity and . . ."

Our reputation is often defined by what we are seen doing; our character by what we are not seen doing.

19 SEPTEMBER

"Weeds. Honesty and integrity, them are weeds, all full of colors and thorns, wicked things."

The power of lies to delude us into believing the very qualities of being that we would most desire, the deepest authenticity, is an enemy and an impediment. The most pernicious lies have the most truth in them.

20

"Ego? That's your benefactor?" He waited until they nodded. "Ego is your boss, then?"

"Yeah," admitted Bluster. "He's stronger than we are and tells us what to do. He is not going to be happy about us bringing you to meet him. He reports direct to the big boss."

Lies are connected. The surface ones owe their existence to others deeper and stronger. We are the slaves of such "benefactors."

21

"And who is that big boss?" asked Tony.

A sly grin passed across Bluster's face. "Why, you are. Mr. Anthony Spencer, the sorry owner of this excuse for a piece of land, you are the big boss here. I'd watch myself around you, I would. Heartless and conniving, that one."

At the heart of all the little lies is "the" lie: that I would be as god, determining the good and the evil, independent and self-serving.

SEPTEMBER 22

"Just tell me what it is," demanded Tony.

"It's a temple," stated Bluster over his shoulder, and then laughed as if heckling. "You should know, you should. You built it. You worship there."

We are created to worship, so we all do . . . somewhere. We build internal temples to what it is or who it is that we center our lives around.

23 SEPTEMBER

He had paid little attention to the stone edifice when he first entered, but now he was close enough to appreciate how the enclosure was constructed. It appeared fashioned from gigantic boulders fitted together with care and precision, impenetrable and rising hundreds of feet into the air before disappearing into a bank of accumulating low-lying clouds.

The power given to us to be a creator inherently means that we are able to design and construct monstrous habitations of lies.

24

A tall, thin fellow emerged from one of the structures. He looked odd, as if he were built disproportionately. Something was off, and Tony almost wanted to look at him sideways to see him better. It was his head, considerably larger than it should have been in relation to the rest of his body, his eyes a little too small and his mouth a little too wide. A thick layer of makeup, like flesh-colored paste, had been applied to his face.

That which is not authentic is always at least a little "off."

25 SEPTEMBER

As he spoke, the makeup on his face drooped, hanging loosely but not quite falling off. In the spaces that separated, Tony could see what looked to be ugly dark bruises. Tony felt a rush of sickening arrogance, as if he were standing in the presence of someone totally self-absorbed.

"You must be Ego," stated Tony.

The false self I believe is true must work to cover up the real and present damage. Question populates the space between the facade and the hurt.

26

"Why do you exist?" asked Tony, more a demand than a question.

"Why, to help you make decisions," responded Ego, a look of cunning sliding across his broken face. "I remind you of how important you are, how necessary you are for the success of those who feed off you, how much they are in your debt. I help you keep score of the ways they have offended you and the mistakes they have made that cost you. It is my job to whisper in your ear that it is you who counts in the world. Mr. Spencer, you are a very important man, and everyone loves, admires, and respects you."

Sweet words in the mouth of a deceiver eventually leave a bitter aftertaste.

27 SEPTEMBER

"And I don't really deserve their respect or admiration."

"Oh, Mr. Spencer, it pains me to hear you say such nonsense. You deserve all that, and more. Look at all you have done for those people; the least they could do for you is to acknowledge your efforts on their behalf. They owe you that much, at least. . . . Your employees would be out of a job if it were not for you. . . . And still they talk behind your back and plot ways to wrest your authority away from you. They don't understand you. They don't see you as the gift that you are. It hurts me to even think about it!"

"The least they could do . . ."
Such a seductive road . . . to ruin.

28

Tony had voiced these thoughts only to himself. They contained a self-fueling logic, tapping into resentments and bitterness that he now recognized lay behind many of his actions. Confrontation with his own damaged ego was ugly and distorted. "I don't want to be like that anymore!"

Please, dear God, help me see
with clarity what it is that I
no longer want to be.

29

"Mr. Spencer, there is exactly a perfect example why you are such a great man. Listen to the authenticity of your confession. Well done! God must truly be pleased with a follower like you who is so humble and contrite, so willing to lay down self and choose a different path. I am honored to be your friend, to call you brother."

Is there any hope for us? We are broken, and on bended knees we pray our pleas for forgiveness, but then arise and consider how proud we are of our humble expressions. Again, please forgive me.

SEPTEMBER 30

Wasn't Ego right? Didn't God want Tony to change? To repent? But Ego's words had a hint of ugly and wrong, almost like Tony's old agenda was being replaced with a newer one, perhaps shinier, prettier, and more self-righteous. But underneath there was always an expectation, sometimes obvious, often hidden, but always still an agenda, the same performance-based agenda.

"I know what you are," Tony declared. "You are just some uglier and maybe even more honest form of myself!"

Holy Spirit, help me distinguish the flesh from the spirit, light from the dark, and the Truth from the lie.

1 OCTOBER

The Month of Transformatio

"Mr. Spencer, you are right as usual. You must die to yourself, put others and their concerns and issues in place of your own needs and desires and wants. Selfless love, that is the utmost and most beautiful sacrifice and one that God would be greatly pleased with. You must crucify the self, die to self, and put God on the throne of your life. You must decrease so that he"—he pointed up with a skinny finger—"can increase."

How easily lies hide
inside religious language,
baptizing deception.

2

"Don't you see, that is what he wants, for you to become like he is, free." Ego yelled the word, and it echoed off the stone towering overhead. He danced in a slow circle, raising his arms slowly and dropping them while in a singsong voice he declared, "Free! Free to choose. Free to love and live and let live, free to pursue happiness, free from societal and family bonds, free to do whatever you want because you are free!"

How could something that sounds so right be so fundamentally wrong?

3 OCTOBER

"Stop!" bellowed Tony.

Ego froze, standing on one foot, arms akimbo.

"That's what I have been doing already, whatever I want, and it hasn't been freedom at all." Tony's anger surged. "All my 'freedom' did was hurt people and build walls around my heart until I couldn't feel anything anymore. Is that what you mean by freedom?"

I began with a lie, that freedom is a synonym for independence, and soon a cascade of lies is in its wake, and my heart began to turn to stone.

4

"Well," Ego said as he lowered his arms and planted both feet firmly on the ground, "freedom always has its price."

If the cornerstone of our strongholds is a heart of stone, shaped by lies, then what becomes of our edifice of self-protection when the heart begins to turn to flesh?

5 OCTOBER

"Look to Jesus, Mr. Spencer. Your freedom cost him everything! He gave his very life to set you free. This man went to God and cried . . ." Again Ego became theatrical, turning skyward with eyes closed as if in the deepest pleading and intercession toward heaven: "Dear God, pour out all your wrath, all the anger you feel toward this vile and wicked creation . . . Let me bear your cruelty, the just deserts of their wickedness. Burn me with your eternal fire instead of them, that your sword of divine justice that is brandished even now over their heads would fall instead upon me."

Forgive me, Papa God, for so long I believed this about you.

6

Tony pressed the point. "So God poured out all his wrath and anger on Jesus instead of human beings and his wrath and fury were forever satisfied? Is that what you are telling me?"

"He certainly has taken upon himself our suffering and carried our sorrows, but we thought that God had wounded him, beat him, and punished him." Isaiah 53:4

7

"You see, the truth is God is rather difficult to get along with. His creation"—he raised his palm, indicating Tony—"has disobeyed him grievously. As a result, the wrath of God is now a constant part of God's being, like an ever-burning fire, a necessary evil if you would; and it continues to burn with an eternal flame, consuming everyone and everything that does not accept and appropriate what Jesus did. Are you following?"

I confess: I have attributed to you the very things that I despise in myself; self-centered, non-relational, and independent.

OCTOBER 8

"Well, regardless, you must always remember that the one constant about God is his anger and righteous wrath, which he has already fully poured out on Jesus. So if you want to escape the wrath of God, you have to become like Jesus, surrender your life and live like Jesus did, holy and pure. Be ye perfect, even as I am perfect . . . That's in the Bible."

The best lies are filled with truth, especially when Scripture can be quoted to support them. (Luke 4 and Matthew 4)

9 OCTOBER

"So, then," Tony said as he looked at the dry and desolate ground at his feet, "there's no hope for someone like me; that's what you're saying. I don't have what it takes to live like that, like Jesus, holy and pure."

"No, no, that is not true, Mr. Spencer. There is always hope, especially for someone who tries as hard as you, who is as special as you. There is just no certainty, that's all."

If my salvation is even partially and therefore ultimately up to me, there is no certainty.

10

"Then you are telling me that relationship with God is only wishful thinking, nothing to really stand on, just a possibility?"

"Please, don't discount wishful thinking. Almost everything in your world was manufactured by wishful thinking, Mr. Spencer. Don't sell yourself short. In your wishful thinking, your hoping, you become very much like God."

I know I am not a "wishful thought," but I am your intention.

11 OCTOBER

"For God so loved the world . . . ," challenged Tony. It was part of a verse that Tony remembered from somewhere.

Ego dropped his gaze dramatically to the ground. "That is so incredibly sad, isn't it?"

"Sad?" Tony refuted. "It isn't sad. If it's true, it's the most beautiful thing I have ever heard! God loves the world! That means God loves those of us in the world. God loves me!" The realization ignited his anger, which flashed bright, and he embraced it, spewing it on Ego. "You know what? I don't care what you want. You are liars and your lies are demonic . . ."

To the degree that we do not know we are loved, we fear.

12

"A bunch of liars, that's what you are! What right do you have to be here, any of you? I demand to know, by whose authority have you claimed a right to be here?"

"Yours!" echoed a booming voice from inside another building, the grandest in the settlement. Startled, Tony took a step back as the door slowly opened and a huge man stepped out. An odor of pungent waste and sulfur emerged with him. Tony stood stupefied, face-to-face with . . . himself, except much bigger.

I have found my enemy, and it is me!

13 OCTOBER

"Surely you know me. I am your superior self, all that you had hoped and wished to be. It was you, with the help of a few of your benefactors, who empowered you to create me. You fed me and clothed me and over time I have grown stronger and more powerful than even you imagined, and it is now I who have been creating you. Birthed as I was in the deepest recesses of your need, you were first my creator, and I was in your debt, but I have been diligent and have repaid you many times over. I now no longer need you for my existence. I am stronger than you!"

Why do we believe our lies have become more powerful than we who created them?

14

"It was never whether you actually had any true safety or certainty; it only mattered that you believed you did. You have a magnificent power to create reality from suffering and dreams, hopes and despair, to call from within the god that you are. We simply guided you, whispering what you needed to hear so you could realize your potential and create an imagination from which you could manage your world. You survived this cruel and heartless world because of me."

Jesus, I need you to be outside my edifice of lies, the Truth not dependent upon my belief. Then come into my darkness and find me.

15

A curtain was drawn across his sight, and everything clear and tangible over the last few days lost clarity and color. The ground leaked a dark visible poison, rising like loose marionette strings around him, constricting his ability to see clearly and think lucidly. A ravenous despair consumed the delicate pieces of his heart that had begun springing to life and sucked them into the well of deep loneliness that had always scarred his heart. Grandmother vanished. He was alone and blind.

In the midst of the fury of emotions, please remind me that you don't do abandonment.

OCTOBER 16

Then he felt the breath on his face, kissing him with the sweetness of an intoxication. The fragrance pushed out and replaced the foul stench that had dominated. And then he heard the whisper, "You are utterly alone, Tony, just as you deserve to be. It would have been better if you had never been born."

When a lie offers you an easy out, it carries with it a sweetness and intoxication, seductive in its embrace. It kisses like a friend who is about to betray you.

17 OCTOBER

It was true, he thought. He was alone and deserved it. He had killed the love of everyone who had offered it to him, and now he was nothing more than a dead man walking. The admission swept through him like the last crumbling walls of a stronghold. Fingers of icy dread slipped like bands around his chest, penetrating through the flesh, reaching for his heart to squeeze until it no longer beat. He froze, stone from the inside out, and nothing he could do would stop it.

I have felt the kiss of hopelessness, who whispers, "Just give up. The world would be a better place without you." Worst place I have ever been! It was a lie!

18

And then he heard in the distance, but drawing near, the sound of a little girl's laughter and singing.

In all my adult ways, one thing that still can reach me is the sound of a child's laughter and song. That tells me I am not completely lost.

19 OCTOBER

"Is that what you are, Mr. Tony? A hopeless failure?"

A litany of successive images tumbled through his mind, all in support of his self-accusation, validations of the judgment against him.

"Oh, Mr. Tony!" she exclaimed without any sense of incrimination. "You are so much more than that!" It was an observation, not a value statement.

Grace, the whispers of Relentless Affection that sing us into healing.

20

The little girl began to hop-skip around him, moving in and out of his view while touching her fingers in no particular order as if keeping a count. In a singsong voice, she declared, "Mr. Tony, you are also a mighty warrior, you are not alone, you are someone who learns, you are a universe of wonder, you are Grandmother's boy, you are adopted by Papa God, you are not powerful enough to change that, you are a beautiful mess, you are the melody . . ." And with each phrase the ice chains that seemed to bind him loosened and his breathing deepened.

I need others who know who "I am" inside this darkness, and I want to learn to trust them, not just need them.

21 OCTOBER

What did she know? She was just a little girl. Regardless, her words carried power, of that he was certain, and they seemed to resonate in his frozen core. Her presence was like springtime unfolding, the thaw that warmed and invited new things. She stood directly in front of him, leaned in, and softly kissed his cheek.

"What is your name?" He was finally able to find a whisper.

She beamed. "Hope! My name is Hope."

Hope will always find her way!
This is a kiss of life!

22

Hope reached up and lifted his chin until he was looking deep into her incredible eyes. "Fight him, Mr. Tony," she whispered. "You do not fight alone."

"Fight who?"

"Your empty imaginations that raise themselves up against the knowing of the character of God. Fight them."

"How?"

"Get angry and tell the truth!"

Anger is the right response to everything that is wrong!

23

"I am the one who relentlessly loves you," she said, beaming, and stepped back. "Mr. Tony, when you find yourself in the darkness, don't light your own fires, don't circle yourself with a blaze you have set. Darkness cannot change the character of God."

Isaiah 50:10–11. I hear the whisper . . . Grandmother . . . Spirit . . . trust!

OCTOBER 24

"I thought Grandmother left me . . . right in the middle of the battle."

"Never left. Your imagination hid her from view. You were lighting your own fires."

"I don't know how not to do that," confessed Tony.

With every learning there is usually an unlearning.

25 OCTOBER

"Trust, Mr. Tony. Trust. Regardless of what your reasoning or emotions or imagination are telling you, trust."

"But I am so not good at that."

"We know. Trust that you are not alone, that you are not hopeless." She smiled and kissed his cheek again. "Mr. Tony, simply trust your mother's word to you. Can you do that?"

Baby steps. Sometimes it seems to come back to the very basic and simple . . . baby steps!

26

"It only takes the smallest desire, Mr. Tony. Jesus is very good at trusting. He will make up the difference. Like most things that last, trusting is a process."

Sometimes my desire is not much bigger than a mustard seed. You knew that going into a relationship with me, right? Good!

27 OCTOBER

A third time she waltzed her breeze-driven dances in a circle around him and a third time leaned in to kiss his other cheek. "Remember this, Mr. Tony, Talitha cumi." She stepped back, then leaned forward and touched her forehead to his, breathing deep. "Now go," she whispered, "and be angry."

Anger is a beautiful emotion except when it becomes the reason to injure and hurt.

28

"You are a liar!" roared Tony, pointing a finger up at the grotesque image of himself. "I don't need you anymore, and I revoke any right that I have ever given you, any right to have any say or authority in my life, and I revoke it now!"

We have made vows that we must
one day take back, agreements
with lies that must be broken.

29 OCTOBER

"Liar!" yelled Tony with fury. "You have told me these lies all of my life, and it has produced nothing but heartache and hurt. I am finished with you!"

"You are alone," hissed the other. "Who would lower themselves to be with you?"

"Jesus!" It surprised Tony to hear himself say it, out loud. "Jesus!" He said it again and added, "And the Holy Spirit and the Father of Jesus."

In truth you did not lower yourselves at all, but raised me up to be with you.

30

"The Father of Jesus." The hulking creature spit the words. "You hate the Father of Jesus. He killed your parents; he crushed your mother." He took a step closer, gloating. "He murdered your only son, took him screaming and kicking into oblivion. He ignored every prayer you prayed. How can you trust such an evil being who would kill your innocent son like he did his own?"

"I don't!" bellowed Tony, and as he said it, he knew it was true.

For many of us, religion has taught us that behind the back of Jesus lurks an untrustworthy god, a father whom Jesus came to save us from.

31

Tony lowered his gaze, glancing quickly again at Grandmother, who still stood like a statue, unwavering. "I don't know him well enough to trust him, but Jesus trusts his Father, and that's good enough for me."

The false Tony, large and formidable, began to shrink. His features caved in on themselves, his clothing hanging loosely from his body, until he stood a mere shadow of his former self. He became a caricature.

Loving and trusting happen inside knowing. For all I do not know, I can rest inside the trust and faith that Jesus has in his own Father.

1 NOVEMBER

The Month of Quickening

"Good!" declared Tony. "I want you to leave and take all your lying followers with you." The dozen odd-looking creatures who had gathered during the confrontation along with the few he had met glanced nervously in his direction. Most stared their hatred and contempt for their despised leader, now reduced to a sniveling excuse. As their chief had lost his power and authority, so, too, had each of them. Even Bluster and Swagger were flimsy representations of their former selves, and none too happy about it.

Lies have greater power in
the dark than in the light!

2

"Just because you are not able to see something doesn't mean it isn't there." Grandmother chuckled.

I'm beginning to understand that. There are many real things that I see only the effects from, such as truth, or kindness, or love . . . it's like the wind.

3 NOVEMBER

Grandmother reached up and put her hand on Tony's shoulder. "You fought well today, son. But even though these in particular have been defeated, you must be on guard for the echoes of their voices that still remain within the walls of your mind and heart. They will come to haunt you if you allow them."

I would rather that once lies were defeated they disappeared never to return. Please sensitize my heart to know when they approach, especially when they are subtle.

4

"Because you built these facades," Grandmother began, "we will not tear them down without your participation. In one's hurry to knock walls down, one can cause them to fall on those they love. Freedom can become a new justification for disregard and a lack of compassion for the bondages of others. Roses have thorns."

I confess: I don't want to turn my freedoms into ways to hurt and divide others.

5 NOVEMBER

"I don't understand.
Why do roses have thorns?"

"So that you handle them carefully and gently."

Hah! My habit has been to get thicker gloves so I can handle without care. Please forgive me for such callous disregard for what is precious to others.

6

"But they will come down then, someday? The walls?"

"Of course, someday. But creation wasn't spoken in a day, Anthony. Such walls aren't erected overnight either. They were built over time, and it takes time and process for them to come down. The good news is that without the help of all those 'friends' you just kicked off your property, it will be harder for you to keep the facades standing."

I understand that in earthquakes it's the facades that come down that hurt people.

7

"You built these walls to keep you safe, or at least for the imagination of safe. They substitute for trust. You are beginning to understand that trusting is an arduous journey."

True! An arduous journey indeed! One that constantly pulls me out of what I thought "safe" and presenting me with your presence, Someone to trust. Thank you, Jesus, for loving me that much!

NOVEMBER 8

"When you believe that you alone are the only one who can be trusted, then yes, you need these walls. Self-protective measures, intended to keep evil out, often wall it in. What initially kept you safe can eventually destroy you."

"But don't I need walls? Aren't they good things?"

He felt the hug from behind. "You need boundaries," said the voice of Jesus, "but not walls. Walls divide while boundaries honor."

Even perfection comes
with boundaries . . . think Eden.

9 NOVEMBER

"Even in our material creation," continued Jesus, "boundaries mark the most beautiful of places, between the ocean and the shore, between the mountains and the plains, where the canyon meets the river. We will teach you how to thrill with us in the boundaries while you learn to trust us with your security and safety. One day you will no longer need walls."

Please teach me to distinguish between the two and give me the wisdom and courage to know when it is time to let a wall come down.

10

Even as he spoke, Tony could sense more internal walls crumbling. Not disappearing, but tangibly impacted by an inner knowledge that he was utterly accepted, with all his flaws and losses, all his conditioning and pride. Was this love? Was this what it was like to be loved?

The walls we built to keep us safe can only come down when we know who we are.

11 NOVEMBER

Grandmother stood back, beaming. "It's good to hear the changes in your voice," she stated.

"What does that mean?" asked Tony.

"As healing happens in a person's soul, their voice changes, noticeable to anyone with ears to hear."

I always delighted to hear the affirmation of others when I was a child, and now my soul smiles to know that my Father delights in what he is doing in me, pleased, even thrilled with the changes in me.

12

"But . . ." Tony stalled. "Why don't you choose for me? You are divine and all, so you would know better than I do."

Jesus smiled, the wrinkles at the corners of his eyes only adding to their brilliance. "This is about participation, Tony, not about puppeteering."

"So, you . . . trust me with this choice?"

"Absolutely!" Both nodded.

The celebration of and the participation with the "other" is at the heart of relationship.

13 NOVEMBER

"Maggie, lots of us praying for Lindsay, just so you know."

"Thanks, darlin'," responded Maggie. "That is the best gift you can give us right now."

Prayer is powerful presence;
a gift freely given that goes
in all directions.

14

It was almost too much for Tony. He hadn't allowed himself this near a children's hospital room, since . . . It had been many years. He could feel himself withdrawing and fought it. Along with his own emotions came a mix of Maggie's deep and ferocious affection for this teenager, and it joined the battle within him. Slowly, she won. As if her compassion had grabbed his arm as he was going out the door and wouldn't let go, he looked again. He listened. He breathed in. All so terribly familiar.

"Not fair," he whispered, even though only she could hear him.

Sometimes you take me into deep waters.
As long as you hold my hand, I will try not to run.

15

"Some things in this life just don't make any sense. The more you stare at them, the less sense they make."

I want to make sense of everything so that I feel I am in control. Please help me trust that you have all of this in your embrace and that there are some things that are simply senseless.

NOVEMBER 16

This hospital had many Lindsays, and each one of them was the center of someone's life. How could he heal just one of them? Wouldn't it be better if he healed himself? He had connections and access to wealth that could really make a difference, in many lives, not just one. Look at everything that had changed for him, in him. Would Grandmother be angry if he made the choice for himself? She would understand.

When you have left the formulas behind, the number of choices seems to grow. Even the choice to act for yourself may truly be the right direction.

17 NOVEMBER

He would almost succeed in stanching his ebbing resolve but then would watch this little human person, a lifetime of potential experiences in front of her cut short by a feud within her own body. There was no question what he would have done for his own son, but . . . this was not his child.

So, whose child is this?

18

"Dear Jesus, I have no power to fix my love, so I am asking you again for a miracle. Please heal her! But even if you choose to heal her by letting her go home to you, I trust you, I do."

In the event of death itself, Jesus defeated it. In every event of death, the conquering continues.

19 NOVEMBER

"I was a terrible father. The physical presence of a man in the house does not disprove the absence of the father. I was gone, in one sense or other, her whole life."

A child does not know how
not to take the blame.

20

"Tony," she replied, "I've never met anyone that was all bad. Mostly bad, yes, but never all bad. Everyone was once a child, and that gives me hope for people. They just end up bringing to the table what they have and they do what they do for a reason, even if they don't know themselves what it is. Takes time to find it sometimes, but there is always a reason."

When you judge someone, you focus on the mess in their life. When you love someone, you encourage the life in their mess.

21 NOVEMBER

Tony wasn't sure about healing himself anymore. He wasn't sure he wanted this ability to decide that a sick person would live. Who was he to make a decision of this magnitude, even on his own behalf? Now that he was actually here, Tony realized that he hadn't thought this through. Jesus and Grandmother had told him he could heal anyone, but this gift was complicated and starting to feel like a curse. Face-to-face with the choice, he was lost.

It is often easier to bear the cross of having nothing than the cross of having something.

22

"Anyway, I think Tony blamed himself, as silly as that seems now. Then he blamed me. Gabriel was born with low birth weight, which they think is sometimes a contributor and somehow that was my fault, and then he blamed the doctors and God, of course. So did I, for a while, blame God. But I discovered that when you blame God for evil, there is no one left to trust, and I couldn't live that way."

From the Garden our first conversation about God was to blame, the accusation of questionable motives and character darkness. After that, we insisted on being alone.

23

"Yeah." Maggie nodded understandingly. "I found that out, too. You can't trust someone who you don't believe loves you."

Yes, at the heart of it all here is my true issue. When I don't believe you love me, I find it hard to trust you. Please, Jesus, build my understanding of the depth of your love for me. . . build my trust.

NOVEMBER 24

"I still can't believe my dad would ever go to a church. He has rather an unresolved history with religious places."

"Well, maybe that's why we connected. I got a little of that, too. Doesn't mean there isn't some real life and value there, but it sometimes gets a little lost behind all the order and politics and job security and stuff."

Human beings who are mixed bags erect institutions that are mixed bags, expressions of both control and compassion.

25 NOVEMBER

Maggie enfolded Angela in her arms and Tony wept inside Maggie, his face pressed against the window of light through which he saw but could not be seen, his hands trying to reach his daughter who cried, so close but so far away. He sobbed for all the losses to which he couldn't even begin to speak, for all the damage he had done. The regret was crushing, but he embraced it.

"Forgive me." His words barely found voice, and he was gone.

We need to stop apologizing and
begin asking for forgiveness!

26

Perhaps true change increased the space in one's heart, creating openness that allowed for authentic community. Within all the regret and loss there blew a hint of expectancy, an anticipation of something more and coming.

Holy Spirit, I love when unexpectedly there arises something within that is fresh, a promise that what seems to be will not always remain.

27 NOVEMBER

A temple? What would he have to do with a temple? Why would this place have any significance? He knew he was being drawn there; he could almost hear the beckoning of a promise. But there was more. Within the weaving of anticipation there was a thread of dread, of something not right, an uneasiness that seemed to have locked his feet in place and wouldn't let them loose.

There is a timing to our courage. What we have sometimes turned away from for fear it might undo us, we must at some point return to and allow it to undo us.

28

"Have I got some questions for you," he muttered and then grinned to himself. Prayer, it seemed, was simply a conversation inside a relationship.

. . . and conversation is as much about the times of silence and listening as the speaking.

29 NOVEMBER

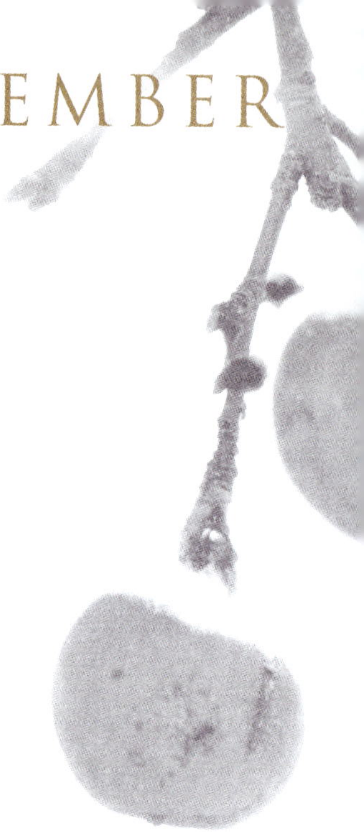

It was the emotional turmoil that accompanied each step. Everything in him screamed go back. Expectancy that had marked the start of the walk dissipated like vapor into a whirlwind of dust that now rose from the riverbed to obfuscate his vision.

When desperation dances with grace, a path will open that before could not be seen.

30

Where in his inner world would a place like this exist? A place of worship! What was a place of worship? It had to be something that he had placed at the center of his life.

We all worship somewhere, each of us a temple and something or someone is seated at the center.

1 DECEMBER

The Month of Letting Go

"Jesus, please help me," he breathed. Whether an answer to his prayer or not, a thought instantly occurred to him. It was like the stillness of morning breaking in the distance and gradually unfolding, but with its clarity came deepening despair. In a moment he knew what this place was. It was the hungering weight at the very core of his existence. It was a tomb, a sepulchre, a grave memorializing the dead.

I confess: I have built memorials to my hurt and pain and losses.

2

Suddenly he saw movement inside the light and froze, gripped in a terror of anticipation. "Gabriel?" He couldn't believe what he saw. What he had feared most and longed for deepest appeared in front of him. It was not an altar, but a hospital bed, surrounded by lights and equipment, and facing him was his five-year-old Gabriel.

There are places, deep and precious, where we got stuck and then built our worlds around. One day there must be a letting go, and what comes down comes down.

3 DECEMBER

"Gabriel, I can't lose you again. I can't!"

"Daddy, I'm not lost. It's you that's lost, not me."

We assume that what we have lost has become lost. Your goodness says otherwise, that you embrace it all and you are not lost.

4

"If only you hadn't . . . died. Why did you have to die? You were so small and weak and I tried to do everything I knew how. Gabriel, I told God to take me instead of you, but he didn't. I wasn't good enough. I'm so sorry, son."

The desperate bargain. We have an innate drive to sacrifice ourselves for someone we truly love. Where did that come from?

5 DECEMBER

"Daddy, please, you've got to stop," whispered his son. "You've got to stop blaming yourself, blaming Mom, blaming God, blaming the world. Please, you have to let me go. You've kept me inside these walls with you for years, and it's time for us to leave."

"You came to me one evening, you forever changed my name, you were the dawn of some new story, and nothing's ever been the same. . . ."

"You put a smile upon my face, that hard times could not erase, you put a song whose tune still lingers, it's a song of love and hope and grace."

6

"Daddy, listen." And now Gabriel dropped to his own knees so he could look straight into the face of his father. "Listen, I don't exist here. You're the one who is stuck here, and it breaks my heart. It's time for you to leave, to be free, to let yourself feel again. It's okay, you know, to really laugh and enjoy life. It's okay."

"You brought me joy when rain was falling,
you made me laugh and cry and pray,
you heard my voice when I was calling.
You always came, but not today. . . ."

7 DECEMBER

"But how can I, Gabriel, without you? I don't know how to let go of you."

"Daddy, I can't explain it to you, but you are already with me; we are together. We aren't separated in the life-after. You are stuck in the broken part of the world, and it's time to be free."

"So I now untie the bowline, let it slip between my fingers, I want to call the ship back to the shore, instead I struggle out a prayer that somehow finds its way through teardrops and my heart cracks in two as I let go. . . . "

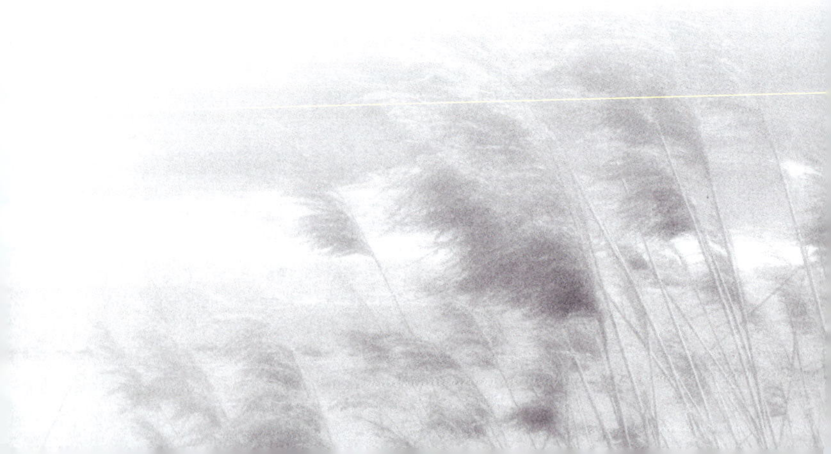

8

"So what am I supposed to do?" Tony could barely get the words out.

"You walk out of here, right through the walls you built, and you don't look back. You let yourself go, Daddy. Don't worry about me. I am better than you can imagine. I am a melody, too."

"If I didn't know your Captain, if I didn't trust his skill, I'd keep you safe at home within our loving arms, but I know you must be going, with the Wind that now is blowing, and I will watch and pray for you, and I will keep a place for you, and I will meet you on some distant shore."

9

Tony turned away, took a deep breath, and began walking toward the wall near where he had entered. With each step, the floor began to crack like stone striking crystal. He dared not look back, certain he would lose all resolve. The barrier in front of him shimmered, then turned translucent and then vanished altogether. He heard a rumble behind him and knew without looking that the temple was caving in on itself, that his soul was heaving with transformation. His steps were now sure and certain.

Tony looked up and saw a monstrous wall of water descending on him. It towered above him and he could do nothing except face it and wait for it to sweep him away. He stood and opened his arms wide. The river had returned.

Bring it on! I need a River to overwhelm me!

DECEMBER 10

"Faith takes risk, Tony, and there is always risk in relationships, but bottom line? The world has no meaning apart from relationships. Some are just messier than others, some are seasonal, others are difficult, and a few are easy, but every one of them is important."

Teach me how to live in such a way that I am an expression that every human being matters!

11 DECEMBER

But being here was right. He could feel it. When Clarence had asked, he had known it was the right thing to do, and it still felt like a good decision. He calmed as he thought about it. When was the last time he had done something for someone else with no strings attached, no agenda? He couldn't remember. Maybe he was trapped, but he accepted it with a sense of satisfaction, maybe even contentment.

When we learn to live without expectations, everything is a gift.

12

"I am not alone here, Anthony. I have lots of company. It's all rather temporary and yet quite permanent. Hard to explain really, how one thing is woven into and yet an extension of another." Her voice was pure and tender, almost like a tune as she spoke. "The body wants to hold on to its connections as long as it is able."

There is beauty embedded even in the losses and the dying. We may not see it clearly, but I am certain that in whatever you have joined me, your presence means there is good.

13 DECEMBER

"Everything I could possibly need while I wait is available to me. All this you see"—her arm orchestrated the air widely as she looked around—"these are my memories that I am cataloging and storing for the time of speaking. Nothing is lost, you know?"

If everything of the cosmos is created in you, Jesus, then there is nothing that cannot be found in you.

14

"Well, that's the wonder: it's not lost. Eternity will be the speaking and celebration of remembering, and remembering will be a living experience. Words," she said, smiling, "are a limitation when trying to speak of such things."

I am finding that words have great limitations, empowered as they are by my perceptions. Please give me new words, new language, new ways to be present without speaking and simply wonder.

15 DECEMBER

"Hush, child, hush now, my baby." She sat down, a small, thin woman holding her man-son in a tender embrace, stroking his head.

Tony cried. Everything he missed about his own mother rose in his memory. But it was a good pain, a right longing, a true connection, and he allowed himself to be carried by its substance.

There are those days of sorrow when I remember and sit in gratitude to those who paid a price to salvage pieces of my heart.

16

Tony was overwhelmed by the holiness of the everyday, the bits and pieces of light that surrounded and embraced the simple routines and tasks of the ordinary. Nothing anymore was ordinary.

When all the religious rhetoric begins to fall away, the formulas of performance turn to dust, there is arising a glory in the ordinary, and I find myself arrayed in joy!

17

"Anthony, I will never be able to thank you enough. This is one of the single greatest gifts anyone has ever given me."

"You are welcome, Amelia, but it really was God's idea. It has been my honor to participate."

It is for participation that we were loved into being. It is our greatest cross and honor.

DECEMBER 18

I met you at the crossing
Where one road finds another
I did not even ask your name
I would not even bother

I looked at only what I saw
And did not see you fall
And even though I said I loved
I hardly loved at all

19 DECEMBER

I didn't mean to leave you there
It wasn't my intent
I simply looked the other way
And said nothing I meant

I didn't choose to cross this road
Although it's what I wanted
Instead pretended you weren't there
Believed you never counted

20

Oh, see I have this golden chain
Tied round my throat and heart
A bond more real to me than you
Is keeping us apart

I need a Voice to answer me
I need Someone who's true
I need new eyes that let me see
That in my me is You

Oh, Someone please now guide me cross
This road betwixt between
And join my broken bits of soul
To real that is unseen

21 DECEMBER

"One never knows if anything's a good idea. You just make a choice and go with the flow and see what happens. You only get one day's worth of grace, so why not spend it extravagantly."

"All right then," he acquiesced. That was a choice he could make, to stay inside the grace of one day. Everything else was just imagination anyway.

That is where I want to live, in a child's simplicity of a single day, and in your Present(ce), Joy has surprised me here.

22

"I have already been dead. Most of my life I've been dead, and didn't even know it. I walked around thinking I was alive and battering everyone in my world with my death. That's not true anymore. I'm alive. For the first time in my life, I'm alive and free and able to make a truly free choice and I've made up my mind. I'm choosing life . . . for me . . . and for Lindsay."

Other-centered, self-giving love!
What is the source of such holiness,
except in you, and when we are
witness to it, we know it as the
deepest True.

23 DECEMBER

Maggie caved in, slumping to the floor in a sobbing heap. In this moment she wanted out, to not be here, to never have prayed that God would allow her to participate in his purposes. The weight of it was a crush, and she almost hated that a light of joy was simultaneously springing inside. The burden of what she had been carrying for Lindsay joined her grief for Tony and together lifted her to her feet.

Your ways are not our ways, and I keep expecting you to do things my way. In these times when nothing seems to make sense, who you are does, and you are where I'm going to run.

24

It is a fragile and thin place, these moments between life and death, and Maggie didn't want to walk without compassion on this holy ground.

Thank you to all you who occupy this space and hold our hands, allowing us to fall apart: Hospice, medical staff, first responders, pastors and priests, counselors and friends . . . thank you!

25

"Well, I'm glad you got to tell him how angry you are. That is a healing thing."

"Me, too. And I'm glad I got to tell him that I love him and that I miss him, too."

Anger is not the enemy of love. In its purest form, it is the deepest expression of love. Jesus comes a tiny baby, the purest expression of God's wrath against all that keeps his creation from being free and knowing love!

DECEMBER 26

"I was destroying the love that I actually had for an imagination of belonging with someone else."

Exchanging what I have for an
imagination of what I might be missing . . .
sounds like a form of insanity.
Please open my eyes to what I have.

27 DECEMBER

"Good-bye, my friend," whispered Maggie, tears spilling down her face as she leaned forward and kissed the man in the bed on his forehead. "I will see you again."

That is the truth . . . on this side of the veil we feel the loss and separation, but what seems from here to be so permanent will not always be.

28

What mattered in this moment to Tony was simply being here, inside the relationship with these two. There permeated in his soul an exhilaration and calm, a settled expectancy and wild anticipation clothed in peace.

There is a settled easiness when I begin to embrace more fully the nature of your love for me. It is everything and more than I have ever hoped and longed for.

29 DECEMBER

"Hey," he wondered aloud. "Where are your places? I don't see either the ranch house or your . . ."

"Hovel," grunted Grandmother. "Never really needed them. All of this is now a habitation, not just bits and pieces. We would never have settled for less."

The purposes of God, expression of the grandest love, have always and ever had "you" at the center. You are the temple of the Living God.

30

"Imagery," added Grandmother, "has never been able to define God, but it is our intention to be known, and each whisper and breath of imagery is a little window into a facet of our nature. Pretty cool, eh?"

Thank you for all the ways you reveal yourself and pursue with Relentless Affection that I have not the power to dissuade.

31 DECEMBER

"It is time for the celebration, the life-after, the gathering and the speaking," answered Jesus, "and just to be clear, Papa has never not been here."

"So now what?"

"Now," said Grandmother triumphantly, "now, the best comes!"

Indeed!

Contributors to These Reflections

There are always a myriad of voices that have spoken into these reflections—some from centuries past, others from just the other day, but all living and significant. Thank you! The following are those who specifically offered a thought or word or poem or song that was woven somewhere into this volume of reflections.

Alexandra (Lexi) Young (OR)—a "young" poet who is wise beyond her years, is not at peace with the surface explanation, but wants to know the deeper. She helps bridge the gaps between people and their hearts.

Amy Young (OR)—an insightful and powerful "young" woman, deeply passionate about all things true. Her perspectives are sure and solid and her call of justice deep and enduring. She is a warrior, strong on behalf of the weak, quick to forgive and stand inside the gap.

C. Baxter Kruger (MS)—my good ol' boy, southern Mississippi theologian friend, who earned his Ph.D. in Aberdeen, Scotland. He's written a bunch of books, including the brilliant *The Shack Revisited* (winter 2012). You can find him at www.thegreatdance.org.

Danny Ellis (NC)—Irish singer-songwriter, responsible for creating one of my all-time favorite albums, *800 Voices* (soon to be a book and stage production). He is David Wilcox's voice teacher . . . just saying. You can find much more of Danny at www.dannyellismusic.com.

David Garratt (NZ)—elder Kiwi statesman, who along with his wife, Dale, created *Scripture in Song* and had a huge impact on praise and worship music in the '60s and '70s. David shares my heart for indigenous cultures and their unique contributions. The Garratts are the truest of friends. More at www.davidanddalegarratt.com.

John MacMurray (OR)—my friend, a theologian and professional nature photographer whose work has adorned the pages of such prestigious magazines as *National Geographic* and *Sierra Club*. You can find some of his work at www.creationcalendars.com. Also check out www.opentableconference.com.

Michelle Young (WA)—daughter-in-law and mother of some of the most incredible and significant grandchildren in the universe, like yours, of course. A woman of deep and quiet courage, determined to find the right, the beautiful, the real, the true, the most genuine . . . and to craft her own soul to be a place of thankfulness!

Pam Vredevelt (OR)—skilled clinician inside the world of damage done, especially to children. Mother of Nathan, who is Cabby in *Cross Roads*. A woman of character who by her presence makes us all want to be "more" than we are today, and yet at rest with where we are so far.

Ron Graves (OR)—Irish Catholic man's man, who played semipro rugby for a quarter of a century, a blue-collar prayer veteran, who writes poetry and keeps the most beautiful journals I have ever seen full of art and words that keep me grinning. Ronnie, you are my friend.

And as always, a loving nod to Canadian singer-songwriter **Bruce Cockburn**, the artist's artist whose lyrical genius is inevitably lurking somewhere inside my words. He has his own Canadian postage stamp! www.brucecockburn.com

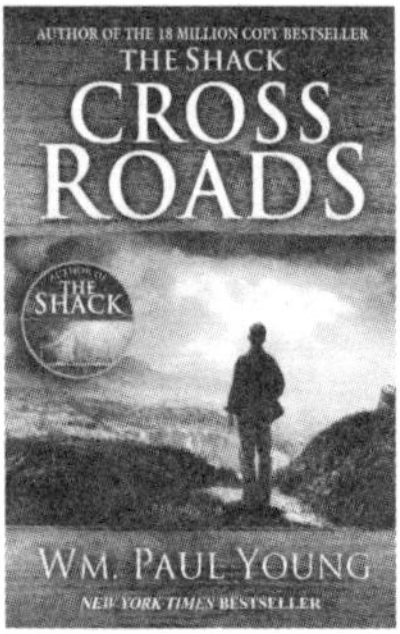

A cerebral hemorrhage leaves egotistical multi-millionaire Anthony Spencer in a coma. He “awakens” to find himself in a surreal world pulsating with a “living” landscape that mirrors the waste and loss of his earthly life. But to his amazement, he is given a second chance. He is sent on a journey back to earth, but one that will enable him to redeem himself only by using the literal “eyes” of several individuals through which he can experience their world view, their hopes and concerns, and their trials. Each of these different experiences has the potential of contributing to Tony’s redemption. But there is a catch: Tony must use a special power he’s been granted to physically heal one person. He can even heal himself. Will he have the courage to make the right choice and thereby undo a major injustice he set in motion before falling into a coma?

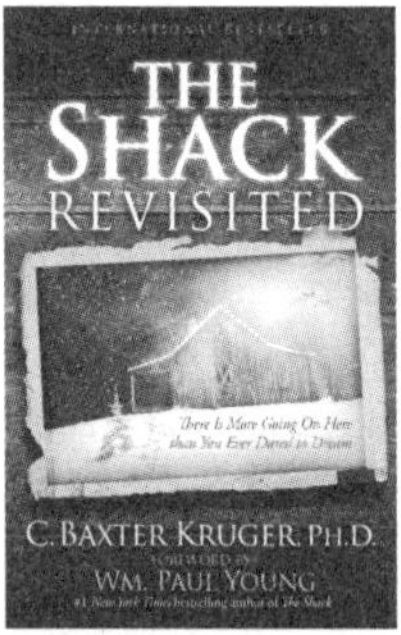

We invite you to continue your experience with *Cross Roads Reflections* by reading *The Shack*, the book that introduced the world to Mackenzie Phillips, Papa, Sarayu, and Jesus; *The Shack Revisited* by C. Baxter Kruger (foreword by Wm. Paul Young), the book that guides readers into a deeper understanding of God the Father, God the Son, and God the Holy Spirit and helps readers have a more profound connection with the core message of *The Shack*—God is love, and *The Shack: Reflections for Every Day of the Year*, a year-long devotional with meaningful prayers and scriptures hand-selected by Paul Young.